The Feminization of Quest-Romance

The Feminization
of Quest-Romance

Radical Departures

by Dana A. Heller

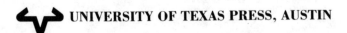 UNIVERSITY OF TEXAS PRESS, AUSTIN

First Edition, 1990

Requests for permission to reproduce material from
this work should be sent to Permissions, University of
Texas Press, Box 7819, Austin, Texas 78713-7819.

♾ The paper used in this publication meets the
minimum requirements of American National
Standard for Information Sciences—Permanence
of Paper for Printed Library Materials, ANSI
Z39.48-1984.

Library of Congress Cataloging-in-Publication Data

Heller, Dana A. (Dana Alice), 1959–
    The feminization of quest-romance : radical
departures / by Dana A. Heller. — 1st ed.
        p.   cm.
    Includes bibliographical references and index.
    ISBN 0-292-77048-0 (cloth : alk. paper). —
ISBN 0-292-72471-3 (pbk. : alk. paper)
    1. American fiction—Women authors—History
and criticism.   2. Women and literature—United
States—History—20th century.   3. Feminism
and literature—United States—History—20th
century.   4. American fiction—20th century—
History and criticism.   5. Romances—
Adaptations—History and criticism.   6. Heroines
in literature.   7. Quests in literature.   8. Women
in literature.
I. Title.
PS374.W6H43   1990
810.9'9287'09045—dc20   90-12619
                                          CIP

Contents

Acknowledgments

Various forms of institutional and individual support have helped bring this text into being. I am gratefully indebted to the following for contributions, guidance, and encouragement generously provided: The Graduate School and University Center of the City University of New York; my parents, Dorothy and Edwin Heller; Rosemary C. Masters, who persistently asked the right questions and listened while I groped for answers; Gerhard Joseph, my dissertation advisor; Morris Dickstein and Mary Ann Caws, who offered feedback and advice; Frankie Westbrook, my sponsoring editor at the University of Texas Press; and J. T. Eckhoff, who put theory into practice.

Moreover, I want to thank Claire Pamplin for her openhearted insight and abiding good humor. This work is dedicated to her with love.

1. Introduction

The Feminization of Quest-Romance

Things are starting to be written, things that will constitute a feminine Imaginary, the site, that is, of identifications of an ego no longer given over to an image defined by the masculine . . . but rather inventing forms for women on the march, or as I prefer to fantasize, "in flight," so that instead of lying down, women will go forward by leaps in search of themselves.   **—CIXOUS, "CASTRATION OR DECAPITATION?"**

Questing, a woman dares to reinvent herself. Unfamiliar, indiscreet, she "lights out" into strange continents, collecting out of the darkness stories never heard before. She moves against the winds of great legends that recount the adventures of heroes, gallant men whose stories are deemed universal, timeless, and fundamental to our understanding of the historical conditions that gave rise to civilizations. In the myths and rituals of Western patriarchal culture, woman is expected to know only what the dominant ideology occasions her to know, and she develops in relationship to this complex illusion which fixes her within the limits of someone else's desire. Indeed, she may reject these limits, refuse to become self-sacrificing, submissive, dependent. Yet this rejection alone does not fulfill her need for an empowering self-image, nor does it grant her the mobility she requires to imagine, enact, and represent her quest for authentic self-knowledge.

Emerging from her entrapment in subservient roles, the woman who rejects the passive term "heroine" and adopts the active term "hero" for her own identity appropriates power from the masculine sphere and accepts the active disobedience of patriarchal law and language. "In the picture language of mythology," writes Joseph Campbell in *The Hero with a Thousand Faces*, "[woman] represents the totality of what can be known. The hero is the one who comes to know."[1] As the male hero of Campbell's monomyth undergoes trials and moves toward the center of knowledge, woman may assist or hinder his progress; she appears as the mother whose admonitions the hero must ignore, the wife who remains silently steadfast and heedful, or the maiden who becomes a bride and a trophy for the hero on the successful completion of the quest's cycle. No matter how the hero encounters her, "[woman] can never be greater than himself, though she can always promise more than he is yet capable of comprehending."[2] However, these powers of comprehension are at last discovered to have been within the hero from the very start. In Campbell's view, women are accessories for the male's heroic adventure. The hero's journey to full masculine adulthood requires that he acknowledge and master the feminine side of his own nature, embrace what Carl G. Jung termed the *anima*. The cycle of the quest celebrates masculine superiority, the triumph of the male's assimilation of the female, the union of *anima* and *animus*, the feminine moon and the masculine sun. What the process reveals is the male hero's uncompromised self-sufficiency in the world, his embodiment of the universal cycle of birth, initiation, and death.

Although in his later writings Campbell restored archetypal powers to the lives of women, his analysis of transcultural myth in *The Hero with a Thousand Faces* proceeds from many of the same ideas regarding the feminine that Jung developed in his theory of archetypal images. Emphasizing male archetypes as universal vehicles of agency and power in narrative, Jung privileges male psychology. In his definition of masculine versus feminine attributes, Jung sets up rigid boundaries that have provoked doubts as to the difference between the function of archetypes and stereotypes.[3] And while followers of Jung have been quick to defend their critical methods by claiming that no archetypal categories are meant to be absolute, the unconscious self that is symbolized by Jung's masculine hero "manifests itself empirically as the sum total of *all* [italics mine] archetypes . . . ," and therefore presumes that all cultural myths spring from male experience.[4]

The birthright of the hero is a voice that speaks not only for a community, but for whole nations, or even planets. The quest affirms the hero's essential individual service to the collective whose salvation rests in his hands. However, the hero must sever his ties to the social order before any restoration can be achieved. The resulting paradox has widely recognized significance for human and cultural developmental studies. As Missy Dehn Kubitschek has observed, "Though each quester seeks a place within a community as opposed to a privately defined role, each must journey outward from that community."[5] The successful completion of the rite of passage depends on this realization, as well as on the hero's restoration of life to the community from which he is initially divided. The adventures of the male quester must eventually bring together the individual and the all; traditionally, heroic action teaches the coherence of worldly and spiritual being.[6] The unity that is achieved through the masculine monomyth—warring parties reconciled, day and night balanced, marriage of male and female achieved—parallels the internal unity of the hero as he makes his own inner progress. Through him, and within him, contradictory forces are eventually put to rest, all oppositions are resolved and revealed as essentially a part of the overriding structure of the cosmos. Ultimately, the myth—no matter what culturally specific form it takes—serves as a means to the same end: "to slay the tenacious aspect of the father . . . and release from its ban the vital energies that will feed the universe."[7]

To kill and to restore: the cycle of the quest equates an antagonistic process of individuation with maintaining the universal order. Competition guides the dialectic structure of the quest and defines male heroism as an aggressive destiny achieved through exercise of physical strength. The world provides the necessary stage, a place where one may attain the ultimate boon: manhood. The situation of Hannibal in the Alps sets the terms of "the man who single-handedly conquers the world, makes a road for others to follow, but makes them lesser men in the following and makes other and greater roads more difficult to create."[8] Even when characterized by rebellion against a social order, the story of masculine development privileges the concept of an aggressive libidinal drive and individuation achieved through victory over all rivals. The hero may then return to his community—which is now the better off for his having succeeded—claim his throne, and be heralded as the heir apparent. But the continuation of the life cycle demands that heroes win their laurels only to be displaced by new heroes, perhaps their own sons. Indeed, it is a condition of the quest that every voyage, "however successful or heroic, has sooner or later to be made over again."[9] The masculine myth thus rejuvenates cultures by making room for new solitary leaders to emerge, individuate from the tribe, kill their predecessors, and assume, finally, an eternal name in the perpetuation of cultural and literary paternity.

According to Northrop Frye, this archetypal "mythos" is fundamentally rooted in both rituals and dreams. As an analogue for the development of the psyche, the quest-romance represents the libido's search to embrace external reality, and at the same time salvage the inner self from the anxieties that accompany that reality. Always subordinate to the masculine libido, woman "achieves no quest herself, but she is clearly the kind of being who makes a quest possible."[10] Clearly, in the critical and psychological assessment of the form women may inspire heroes, but they may not aspire to become heroes themselves; they may serve to symbolize various aspects of the masculine drive, but they may not select new symbols to represent their own desires. The prescribed patterns of the quest would appear to indicate that identity *is* an exclusively masculine attribute. Women's roles remain significant only in relation to the heroes whose identities they strengthen: they have no desires except to be chosen and adored by heroes. The Oedipal division of active and passive roles which defines the drama of traditional quest plots has been succinctly described: "the son against the father for the mastery of the universe, and the daughter against the mother to *be* the mastered universe."[11]

The poet-heroes of late eighteenth- and early nineteenth-century quest-romances conceive of this Oedipal dilemma as an internalized journey. Harold Bloom translates the anxiety of poetic identity into the "anxiety of influence," which sends the hero (the poet) off on a solitary mission (the writing of the poem) to compete with—and ultimately discover within himself—the "Great Original" poet. In terms of the hero's relation to altered economic and scientific conditions, the quest "becomes chivalric jousting transformed to meet the conditions of a social system in which power manifests itself no longer in physical strength, but in the strength of various kinds of cognitive and metaphorical exchanges."[12]

Tracing the path of this transformation in "The Internalization of Quest-Romance," Bloom observes that in the phenomenon known as Romanticism the search turns inward to explore the landscape of the poet's own ego: "The internalization of quest-romance made of the poet-hero a seeker not after nature but after his own mature powers, and so the Romantic poet turned away . . . from nature to what was more integral . . . within himself."[13] The paradox of the romantic quest exists in the hero's troubled recognition of a debt owed the real world, his literary forebears, as he struggles to achieve through the creative process a truly confirmed, individuated masculine selfhood.

In the internalized quest, the poet attempts to overcome the libidinal, feminine self by engaging it in locked battle with the Imagination, or "Real Man." In the triumph of the Imagination, the poet marries the halves of a divided self; an authentic poetic genius is at last united with his muse.[14] Bloom's view of the female's service to the adventure agrees with Frye's "ambivalent female archetype," which exists primarily to affirm the life process that the hero's actions express. In the process of quest-romance, the hero is set against the father, who threatens the younger poet in his courageous efforts to master the divided inner self. The latter's eventual success constitutes his gift to the world, a potential for masculine self-possession and self-resolve more powerful than the anxiety of influence and the impositions of a crude, capitalist social system.

The Romantic poets took the dialectic of self and world, and privileged the former—the internal arena—as that which contained the true drama of the quest. In other words, it was demonstrated that a hero need not slay dragons, fight wars, or traverse oceans in order to attain heroic status. Although internalized quest-poetry of the Romantic period remains, as Marlon B. Ross effectively argues, caught up in "patriarchal conceptions of writing" that reduce women to man-made images entrapped in male fantasies, the internalization in some manner anticipates the feminization of the form by creating a kind of heroism not determined by physical strength but by intellectual and visionary endeavors.[15] Women's social roles, which confined them physically and emotionally to the imperatives of family, marriage, and home, granted them little activity beyond the tedious exercise of domestic chores or polite social pleasantries. Even less were they free to move about in the world independently. Romantic internalization confirmed that the individual mind could be as vast and as challenging as the world; it, too, contained its own antagonists and its own courageous heroes. If, as Bloom suggests, the internalization of the quest emblazoned the creative process itself, there would seem to be nothing to prevent women from becoming heroes themselves by virtue of possessing their own minds and their own imaginative faculties.

However, since women writers became a recognized presence in the literary marketplace, and since they began representing female experience in culturally available narrative forms, surprisingly few genuine female "heroes" have come into existence. Although we may speak of Jane Austen's Emma Woodhouse or Susan Warner's Ellen Montgomery as important literary "heroines," noteworthy precursors to the shift in consciousness that I have termed the feminization of quest-romance, it is difficult to discuss these female protagonists in terms of their independent visions and heroic powers of self-possession. These women remain entrapped by social restrictions and definitions of female "goodness" that demand their passivity, submission, and obedience.

Indeed, after examining quest patterns in over three hundred novels by women, one critic reports that "even the most conservative women authors create narratives manifesting an acute tension between what any normal human being might desire and what a woman must become."[16] Trying to break free of such limitations, trying to work themselves actively into heroic patterns, female questers have been faced with a nearly impossible assignment. And what feminist critics have discovered is an absence of a heroic female self-image. Women have been blocked from identifying themselves with the active subject of quest-romance because they have internalized an image of themselves as passive objects, framed by the classic structure of the myth, removed from the very symbols and activities the quest traditionally evokes.

♋

American literature has engaged in its own struggles to define heroism in accordance with a national identity often characterized by a split between internal desire and external reality. In works by many of America's most time-honored novelists, the quest has been manifested in a youthful hero's effort to enact an initiation into adulthood while clinging desperately to an idealized image of impulsive, chaotic freedom—a state of being that Ihab Hassan has termed "radical innocence." Whether "lighting out" for the territory, hunting the white whale, playing hooky from school, or recklessly engaging life

"on the road," the protagonists of American quest-romance participate in a major tradition relevant to both a general human mythology
and to the specific historical and social conditions of American culture. According to Richard Chase, these conditions are recognizably
expressed in "the perception and acceptance not of unities but of
radical disunities," contradictions that have shaped the American
literary imagination from its earliest emergence.[17] The conflict of
utopian visions—the inimitable "City on a Hill"—with the individual isolation countenanced by early Puritan doctrine; the opposition
and fear that proscribed racial integration from the earliest con-
frontations of native Americans and European whites; the intellectual schism between traditional and progressive social values, or
"Old" versus "New" World—all of these factors contribute to the
dualistic impulse that has shaped American literature and to the
adoption of the romance as our native novelistic form.[18]

Chase's thesis hinges on what he considers to be a misunderstand-
ing on the part of many critics, such as D. H. Lawrence. The preva-
lent misperception holds that the mission of American literature has
been to resolve conflicts and achieve the kind of unity that the masculine quest, in its formal analysis, expresses. On the contrary,
Chase points out, the best examples of our literature ("best" refer-
ring to traditionally canonical works by Hawthorne, Melville, James,
etc.) seek not to resolve oppositions but "to discover a putative unity
in disunity," to search for a place of "rest . . . among irreconcil-
ables."[19] American literature is validated not by an end, but by a
means of discovering forms capable of containing these irreconcilable forces.

Judging from the prominent position occupied by questing male
protagonists in the American canon, we would appear, indeed, to be
a nation as obsessed with "radical disunities" as with masculine images of ritualized flight and self-exploration. As Judith Fetterly has
noted, the pervasive male disposition of American literature equates
the very essence of what it means to be American with the essence of
what it means to be male.[20] Masculine self-development may take
precedence over social integration, or, in more modern quests, both
concepts may be lamented as futile. The hero's vision of personal
achievement may be unholy in the eyes of his community, but
through the rituals of heroic initiation, the toils of conflict, the shak-
ing off of demons bent on obstructing his path, he may still succeed

in attaining heroic status. Social power and autonomy is the reward granted the hero who successfully completes the quest and survives the process of masculine initiation. However, even when a hero rejects the notion of completion—or even when initiation is seen as an impossible task—he may still become heir to the power granted in refusal and heroic failure. If his efforts do not lead to successful social integration, he becomes our admired American anti-hero, our Huck Finn, on the lam from civilization, or our Holden Caulfield, who "lights out" for an inward territory, the field of the restless, solitary psyche.

Post–World War II American fiction has inherited these impulses. In works by contemporary male writers such as Jack Kerouac, Norman Mailer, Ralph Ellison, Vladimir Nabokov, Thomas Pynchon, John Barth, E. L. Doctorow, John Updike, Barry Hannah, and Raymond Carver, there lives a restless wanderlust which American tradition has affirmed as "manly" and which esteemed American critics such as Leslie Fiedler have deemed essential to an understanding of our national spirit—a dislocated spirit always, it seems, defining itself "in flight" from inhibitive social conventions, full genital (heterosexual) maturity, and the domesticating figure of woman. While Fiedler mocks the male-bonding aspects of this character, Hassan's formulation of a new romantic figure extols the "hero of mournful or roguish mien," who "fulfills his destiny by mediating the contradictions to which we are heir."[21] This process of mediation, according to Hassan, occurs most often within the context of a hero's quest for self-discovery. On the run, searching for an authentic sense of selfhood, these characters define the role of the modern anti-hero, the social misfit. No matter how futile his gestures for salvation, no matter how demoralizing his initiation, the male hero remains heroic by dint of the mobility and capacity for action granted him by gender. Even if he remains outcast, he remains also in possession of an active, articulated will: he determines a subject position in the world, and he searches of his own volition. The American anti-hero of quest-romance thus forges—in terms specific to our own cultural landscapes—"a map of the mind and a profound faith that the map can be put to saving use."[22]

What then can be said about a woman's attempt to map the female psyche? Certainly, as Carol Christ recognizes, "the quest motif, which has a long history in Western literature, appears in different form in the new literature written by women. . . . if the hero has a thousand faces, the heroine has scarcely a dozen."[23] She and Annis Pratt agree that, although many female quests share certain elements in common with male versions, they nevertheless reveal their own distinct problems, themes, and motifs. The exploration of these problems and the working through of these themes in women's literature has led to the development of a separate tradition of quest-romance, a distinct history of female heroes and an equally distinct, although more recent, feminization of the quest form which has made viable woman's unique pattern of human development. Over the course of nearly two hundred years, women's quest-romances have contributed to our recognition that woman's experience in patriarchal culture and her limited opportunities for social development have had a direct and lingering influence on her own image of female character. Also directly influenced are the forms women use to convey these images, as well as the critical judgments that readers of both sexes bring to bear upon stories that attempt to speak authentically in woman's own voice.

With that I would offer a word of explanation: in the chapters that follow I refer to the female protagonists of the quest as "heroes," and I am aware of the implicit contradiction which some readers may interpret as an erasure of the female subject. My intention, however, is to join in the recent effort to redefine heroism from a female perspective. At the head of this endeavor, Lee R. Edwards has argued that heroism is mythologically defined as an "asexual or omnisexual archetype" and may be used in relation to men and women.[24] Rachel Brownstein summarizes the more traditional distinction between "hero" and "heroine": "The paradigmatic hero is an overreacher; the heroine . . . is overdetermined. The hero moves toward a goal; the heroine tries to be it. He makes a name for himself; she is concerned with keeping her good name."[25] My definition of female heroism agrees with Edwards's androgynous concept and refers not to the passive female object, but to the active female subject of quest-romance.

♋

Katherine Dalsimer's *Female Adolescence* describes the opening scene of Muriel Spark's *The Prime of Miss Jean Brodie* in a way that would seem to preclude female heroic destiny by curtailing female mobility:

> Outside of the Marcia Blain School for Girls, a small group of boys has stopped to talk—but they stand on the far side of their bicycles, establishing a protective fence of bicycle between the sexes. The boys as they talk, lean on their handlebars, as if to make clear that at any moment they may be off. The girls band close together. The scene suggests immediately the unease, the mutual apprehension between the two sexes . . . the boys poised and ready for flight, the girls huddled together, aware of their imminent departure.[26]

While Dalsimer chooses this scene wisely to evoke the condition of early adolescence, it illustrates precisely the point of departure where a capacity for male and female quest-romance is defined and destinies diverge into two, separate paths. The male hero who ventures out into the world is self-determining and active. His imminent departure is defined by such symbols of flight from the female as the boys' bicycles in the passage just quoted. In contrast, female socialization is marked by a conflict between an equally strong desire to take flight and the social imperative of the "huddle," or engulfing group. Recognition of this difference signals the starting point for the feminized quest and for this study, for while a man's departure is seen as "imminent," a woman's motion toward the door—like Nora's last dramatic act—occasions a radical departure from the "doll's house" of social and literary convention alike. As the male hero defines himself through such symbolic rituals as the quest, achieving his position in the world through hands-on encounters within a social milieu, the young woman's call to adventure must somehow transcend the limits of an enclosed space: a house, a garden, an institution, an introspective mind. Her call to adventure often becomes, in Susan J. Rosowski's words, "an awakening to limitation," a recognition that society neither expects nor wants her to test her powers, prove her autonomy, or step outside the line of "proper" feminine behavior.[27] In short, she realizes that the quest is not meant for her active heroism, but for her passive submission to a hero. The tragic illnesses, suicides, and mental deterioration with which these stories so often end speak of a culture, as well as a male-dominant tradition of literary forms and themes, that has privileged the myth of male flight and denied female protagonists the experience of "lighting out" for a feminized territory of self-creation and social fulfillment.

The perpetuation of this denial stems from an absence of tradition and contexts for female heroes. An equally important factor is that women have traditionally lacked the power to represent themselves publicly, let alone represent the public through heroic endeavor. Female heroines of nineteenth-century women's fiction are often confined to a domestic sphere, conflicted by longings to move beyond the very limits that convey their state of mind. Male heroes, on the other hand, are afforded a more expansive sphere in which to develop. Additionally, gender bestows upon men the privilege of representing whole communities, whole nations, or "mankind."

In order for the cycle of the quest to be complete, these broader interests of the community must at last be served by the hero's adventures. Traditionally, the male myth reinforces the privileges and principles of patriarchal culture, thus delivering the hero back into a world where he may inherit his share of power and benefit from the restoration of the masculine hierarchy. Women's quests, too, must benefit the larger community and reach for an essential connectedness between the individual and her world. However, if her world is one where only men hold power, the female protagonist serves best who stops her quest. "And they stop by marrying," observes Rachel Blau DuPlessis, "often this stops them."[28] Her point is that female heroism may backfire—particularly in nineteenth-century quest-romances informed by marriage plots—by reinforcing customs that empower patriarchy and consequently serve the very principles that keep women in their "proper" place. Women's quests that seek resolution through marriage often signal the female protagonist's recognition that individual aspirations and desires are impossible to achieve outside the institutions which she had once hoped to transcend. Thus, it can be argued that novels such as *Jane Eyre* and *Middlemarch* ultimately relieve their female protagonists of their quests while doing little to open new possibilities—new futures—for the community at large, or for the community of women.

Although by no means exclusive to female quests, conflicts between autonomy and dependence, world and home, rebellion and submission, active and passive behavior, and internal and external exploration are recurrent obstacles to their growth. Rebellion against an oppressive feminine standard that obstructs their journeys toward self-knowledge occurs frequently in the form of internalized combat against an enemy that lives within the female psyche. The demands of patriarchal culture, which female protagonists internalize through "successful" socialization, inevitably must be won over if the female hero is to succeed in her quest. Fighting patriarchal standards, female protagonists may thus engage in a kind of internalized self-combat. The decipherable patterns of inner turmoil described in the overwhelming majority of novels of female development reflect the lack of any outward expression of female aggression. Fetishized, vilified, and codified by a system of male-defined conventions and standards, the would-be hero who remains faithful to unauthentic images of female selfhood is led ever deeper into self-denial, passivity, and inertia.

These "public images that defy reason and have very little to do with women themselves" have been responsible for American women's historical lack of power. In *The Feminine Mystique*, Betty Friedan describes a division of women's self-image which indicates an internalized drama in the psychic lives of contemporary, middle-class American women. Pointing to the classic split between the pure and fair woman whom men worship and the dark, sinful lady who constitutes the object of male sexual fantasy, Friedan discerns a "new feminine morality story" in modern woman's quest for an image of her own. The trials of the quest involve "the heroine's victory over Mephistopheles . . . first in the form of a career woman . . . and finally, the devil inside the heroine herself, the dream of independence, the discontent of spirit, and even the feeling of a separate identity."[29]

One of the difficulties women face in battling the demons both outside and within the psyche is that they must let go of "femininity" in the way that it has traditionally governed female behavior and destiny. Friedan and other feminist writers of the postwar era assert that women's images have not been shaped by women themselves but by men, to perpetuate male power. As soon as a female protagonist becomes the subject of the quest she sacrifices this man-

made aspect of her identity. Her feminized search requires an authentic, "private image," an image that will ultimately benefit both
the individual woman and a society where men and women hold
equal power. Woman's quest must propose strategies for escaping
debilitating structures, for discovering authentic selfhood, and for
claiming the right to take her journey out into the world.

The feminization of quest-romance has evolved slowly, assimilat-
ing influences from both male and female literary traditions. Rejecting contrived public images in favor of personally enabling patterns,
courageous literary protagonists who dared to take their quests out
into the world remained largely unheard of until the twentieth century. The transformation of quest-romance from a form that precludes the female subject to one that speaks directly to woman's
changed position in the public sphere is a clear indication that the
very concept of heroism needs to be critically scrutinized and redefined for a feminized age. Indeed, it is time to map the "dark continent," the frontier of an individual female psyche, while understanding how her specific ties to community, family, and loved ones
empower—rather than restrict—her capacities.

"In order to come back 'for good,' one must go away for a while,"
writes Cynthia Griffin Wolff.[30] The hero who seeks to open new territories of social possibility by narrowing in on a necessary preoccupation with self defines one of the central paradoxes of traditional
quest-romance. Alternately, the hero who enables self-discovery
through the forming of nurturant, reciprocal bonds with others defines the central paradox of the female version of the form. Women's
quests must be able to embody the opposite impulses of separation
and connection. Their journeys must affirm the need to reroute heroic destiny through these paradoxes of female psychic development:
How is a capacity for both autonomy and relationship, attachment
and independence, to be expressed? What forms will explain female
development and embrace these seemingly irreconcilable forces?
The feminization of the heroic quest has provided women writers a
narrative means to acknowledge and accept indeterminate processes
that the masculine myth attempts to determine through rituals of closure, aggression, exclusion, and individuation—rituals that help
preserve an exclusively masculine domain.

The feminization of the quest begins in a word: "No." The female subject assumes the task of continuing to say no to domination, of continuing to speak in her own voice even when she fears that no one will comprehend her. Her fear is understandable, for her voice emerges always in relation to a historical absence that precedes her, an absence from which she still must proceed. The task of the feminist critic, according to Fetterly, is to become a searching reader who says no, "a resisting reader rather than an assenting reader." Feminist criticism, which has concerned itself with reclaiming the voices that were relegated to absence, has begun "the process of exorcizing the male mind that has been implanted in [women]."[31] Simultaneously, it has begun tracing the history of woman's quest for self-definition; these voyages remain a vital expression of woman's need: to set not-hero against hero, to set not-legend against legend, and to create anew.

Thus, the feminization of this process, like the child's earliest articulations of an emergent, self-possessed identity, begins with a refusal that signals the boundaries of self in relation to a responsive "other." Perhaps it is no surprise, then, that this book emerged from what was initially a study of female adolescence in contemporary American fiction. My interests in the contemporary novel of development, or *Bildungsroman*, feminist criticism, and American youth culture led me to explore an American literature of female coming of age. However, as I read, I realized that what interested me was a recurrent pattern less discernible by content than by form. Suddenly, the age of the female protagonist seemed far less important than this form, or motif, which I recognized as a female version of quest-romance.

An established feature of many of these female quests is a thwarted or impossible journey, a rude awakening to limits, and a reconciliation to society's expectations of female passivity and immobility. However, despite this pattern, and despite the difficulty that women writers face in challenging myths, rituals, psychological theories, and literary conventions deemed universal by a culture that valorizes masculine ideals, a number of revolutionary texts have come into existence over the last forty years, all of them working to redefine the literary portrayal of American women's quests. They work, in part, by presenting questing female characters who refuse to accept the roles accorded them by restrictive social norms, even if it means sacrificing themselves in the name of rebellion. In more recent texts, however, these female heroes survive their "lighting out" experiences to explore diverse alternatives to the limiting roles that have proscribed female development.

♋

The title of this book, *The Feminization of Quest-Romance: Radical Departures*, suggests that a female quest is a revolutionary step in both literary and cultural terms; woman's relegation to the private, domestic sphere and her definition in terms of relational and nurturing capacities has made it difficult, if not dangerous, for women writers to present an independent female hero who succeeds without the company or support of men. However, the representations of female quests discussed in my study all manage to strike discordant notes in their own unique efforts to adapt their theme to female experience. What I am interested in is how the quest has been transformed by women writers to express the need for a viable theory of female development and new literary forms to represent this developmental structure. My thesis contends that by tracing the emergence of female quest-romance in American women's writings of the last forty years, we bear witness to its development as one of the most fundamental formal expressions of women's awakening to selfhood, mobility, and influence in the world.

♋

Chapter 2, "Remaking Psyche," looks at several precursory models of female questers and examines some of the issues and influences that emerged from mythical and nineteenth-century engagements of the female quest. In the third chapter, I take up Jean Stafford's neglected classic, *The Mountain Lion*. Stafford's novel is a radical subversion of masculine myth and the traditional American quest-romance. Through a powerful deconstruction of American myth and cultural archetype, Stafford levels a strategic indictment against male-dominant myth and literary conventions that allow no opportunity for the growth of a heroic, independent, and creative female spirit. Examining the novel within the context of the gender dialectic that Stafford constructs and ultimately collapses makes it possible to read *The Mountain Lion* as a novel of social protest leveled against the forces that preclude female heroism in American literature. In my chapter on *The Mountain Lion*, I examine specifically the tactics that the novel uses in its appeal for a more optimistic future for female self-realization.

> The most interesting lives of all, of course, are our own and there is nothing egotistic or unmannerly in our being keenly concerned with what happens to us. If we did not firmly believe that ours are the most absorbing experiences and the most acute perceptions and the most compelling human involvements we would not be writers at all, and we would, as well, be very dull company.[32]

In this statement from "Truth in Fiction," Jean Stafford provides the connection to the fourth and fifth chapters, which examine Mary McCarthy's *Memories of a Catholic Girlhood* and Anne Moody's *Coming of Age in Mississippi*. The outpouring of women's autobiographies since the feminist movement of the 1960s indicates a heightening of public and personal awareness—but, most important, the recognition of the fundamental connection between the two. This awareness has led many notable American women activists and writers to examine their personal lives and aspirations within the scope of their public function. Perceiving themselves as central subjects of family and social history, McCarthy and Moody transform autobiographical narrative into quests that test the boundaries of difference. Although their narratives are dramatically different in form, content, and style, both McCarthy and Moody strive to transcend the internal self-division that Simone de Beauvoir saw in *The Second Sex* as antithetical to women's freedom from patriarchal oppression.

In *Coming of Age in Mississippi*, Anne Moody's search for identity is formed by her active role in the civil rights movement. Affirming her rage against racism and white supremacist policy, Moody explores a territory within herself that many Southern blacks deny for fear of white retaliation. Courageously Moody's quest challenges the boundaries of white and black, the personal and the political; the history of a nation is thus transformed into the history of a young woman's discovery of power within herself and her community.

Mary McCarthy's memoir presents an equally radical challenge to the boundaries of "truthful" representation and the reification of female identity. McCarthy frames each section of her autobiographical fiction with italicized commentary on the objective accuracy of her remembrances. By interrogating herself and her past, McCarthy enacts an inquiry into the origins of self with only language as a means to her discovery. Always in the act of confession, McCarthy negotiates a cognitive position from which to undertake a quest empowered by revision. Her autobiographical journey celebrates a process of rebirth through language, a process of naming one's history and one's self.

My last two chapters deal with recent novels that transform the American romance with life on the road into a theme that redefines the forces of independence and attachment in women's lives. Marilynne Robinson's *Housekeeping* and Mona Simpson's *Anywhere But Here* rework elements of myth, Oedipal theory, and the oppositions of interior and exterior space into new images of female selfhood.

If we place into context the methods and alternatives which these representations of contemporary women's quests propose, it becomes possible to discern a feminized version of the "lighting out" motif that has radical implications for literary values which must continue to change in order to support parallel changes in women's social realities. This revolutionary form, like all modes of communication, interacts with "real" events affecting women's lives. It would be injudicious to read contemporary women's quests without acknowledging the historical forces that gave impetus to the female literary imagination and greatly altered women's perceptions of their social potential and responsibilities. Thus, as Edwards notes, the feminization of quest-romance, like contemporary woman herself, "cannot be understood without some awareness of such matters as divorce laws, suffrage legislation, industrial developments, bills affecting married women's rights to property, access to reliable methods of contraception, and altered economic opportunities."[33] Indeed, the feminized quest has emerged not merely as a trend in women's writings, but as a mediating voice in the social arbitrations of literary form and political reform. Feminist criticism, an emergent cultural force in its own right, has also provided new practical and theoretical contexts for examining women's public functions and understanding their psychic depths.

"Descent returns one to the past," writes Kim Chernin. "It is a time of travel within the self."[34] Descent may lead a woman back in time, in search of lost traditions, lost female heroes. However, descent also leads back to her earliest recollections of the lost goddess in her own life, her mother. Her journey involves not only a motion toward new territories of self-discovery, but a reclamation of the lost self-image that women experience when they come to accept their mothers as weak and their fathers as powerful. Consequently, feminist psychoanalytic theory, which attributes women's developmental "failure" to the rejection of an original figure of female power, provides a useful context for an understanding of contemporary women's quests. Maternal identification theory not only counters the destructive impact of Oedipal models based on Freud's scheme, but also helps illuminate the essential "search for our mother's garden" that informs the female quest. It asks radical questions about models of development that view women's identification with the father as the key to their maturation. It asks whether individuation, in the terms of normalized male experience, is a desirable goal for women, whose object-relational structure tends to see possibilities for inclusion rather than exclusion, sameness rather than difference. While the emphasis on inclusiveness may be thought to perpetuate woman's image as selfless and dependent caregiver, recent theorists such as Nancy Chodorow and Carol Gilligan have demonstrated that her developmental and object-relational difference indicates no failure on woman's part, but society's failure to understand a different process of human growth. To the extent that the feminization of quest-romance is exploring such alternative processes, I believe it also represents Friedan's "turning point from an immaturity that has been called femininity to full human identity."[35]

But the question at the heart of the matter promises no ready answers: What are women searching for? Indeed, we must grant every hero her or his own holy grail even as we look for encompassing patterns and structures for understanding the movement itself. Carol Christ suggests that woman's quest is a mystical, continuous, life-making process that defies conclusion. The power of the experience is derived essentially through its process: woman's spiritual quest leads her through stages of nothingness, awakening, insight, and, finally, an act of self-naming that calls her new identity into being by transforming a relationship between her individual spirit and the world which she inhabits.

And certainly many female protagonists of the new quest participate in this self-naming ritual. In *Betsey Brown*, Ntozake Shange describes her female hero's preparation for running away from home: "Now, what should she call herself for this great journey?"[36] Rejecting Sojourner on the basis that her spirit was "still alive," and Susan B. Anthony because she was white, Betsey decides upon the name Cora. Her choice parallels Julia Kristeva's designation of the semiotic *chora*, a "totality" of nonsymbolic psychic expressions and human drives. Borrowing the term from Plato, who defined it as the the maternal receptacle of all things, an "essentially mobile" and indeterminate articulation, Kristeva posits the *chora* as a signifying mode that is ordered by the mother's body, thus forming "a motility that is as full of movement as it is regulated."[37]

In many of the texts discussed in this study, a preoccupation with the mobility and significance of the female name is apparent: "My name is Ruth," begins Marilynne Robinson's *Housekeeping*. In *Anywhere But Here*, Ann August becomes Heather when she arrives in California. Both *Memories of a Catholic Girlhood* and *Coming of Age in Mississippi* express deep concern over issues of naming, and in the latter case Essie Mae Moody becomes Anne Moody due to an error on her birth certificate. These incidents reflect a characteristic motif of American fiction from Cooper's Leatherstocking novels to *The Great Gatsby*. The name represents a classic dilemma of the American hero, divorced from ancestry, in search of his rightful inheritance. Woman's naming of self, however—much like the Black Muslim ritual of exchanging one's "slave" name for a new identity— is a radically defiant act that assumes a power not generally passed down through the matriarchal line. Unnaming herself, woman not only breaks with the past but with a *patriarchal* past that has deprived women of female-specific identity, history, and inheritance through the matriarchal line. Renaming herself, woman takes possession of Adam's God-given power to name the animals. She rewrites history from her own perspective.

While the feminized ritual of self-naming contributes to the "transformation of the hierarchical mentality" which Carol Christ takes to be an object of women's quests, her analysis is inconsistent. Stating the goal as she sees it, Christ asserts that "women's quest is for a wholeness in which opposition between body and soul, nature and spirit or freedom, rationality and emotion are overcome."[38] And yet, ironically, Christ's own argument is built upon a basic division of female experience into "spiritual quests" and "social quests," a division that is, I believe, incompatible with a thorough understanding of women's cognitive and psychological goals.[39] Although she acknowledges that spiritual quests invariably call forth social objectives in their course, Christ implies that women's exclusion from the latter is somehow "natural," a condition of her psychic strength rather than her cultural acclimation. This implication serves to further dissociate women from the public domain rather than assist in our understanding that human "wholeness" is at best an expression of the dialectic between an individual spirit and her society.

The feminization of quest-romance involves, as is evident in works by contemporary women writers, an effort to hold both these spheres in tension, just as Kristeva's *chora* holds both mobility and stasis in tension. This opposition speaks for the moral dialectic of the feminized quest, inclusion opposed to exclusion; as Carol Gilligan observes, "Although inclusion is the goal of moral consciousness, exclusion may be a necessity of life . . . enabling women to consider it moral to care not only for others but for themselves."[40] This tension addresses as well the relation of the domestic and the public sphere, or home and the world. Paralleling the shift from paternal to maternal identification that forms the psychological core of feminized quests, contemporary American women writers have begun to locate a shift of female power from the home to the world. Consequently, this study will gauge the importance of spatial metaphors in women's psychic development and their visions of personal and public activity.

Women's quests that are directly concerned with the female's relationship to the public sphere often present female heroes pitted against indifferent and immoral antagonists, or powerful yet unjust social institutions. Stepping into activist roles, these women at first appear more like mouthpieces than heroes, but their radical departures may ultimately involve more of a sacrifice of audience than a destruction of malicious forces. What this pattern implies is a system of values that continues even today to tie woman to the imperatives of nurturance and service; however, when woman expresses herself genuinely through such service, she ultimately serves both herself and the futures of all women by breaking down the barriers that divide genderized spheres. The power of the female quester may thus be defined by her ability to use the currency of the maternal sphere in the objective, paternal world.

The Feminization of Quest-Romance is thus a study concerned with woman's desire to "light out" and with what happens to women who do so. The feminization of the heroic quest suggests an essential process by which culture, as well as language itself, is reimagined so that when we say "female," we say "person."[41] As one reads contemporary women's quest stories, it becomes clear that what we are witnessing is no less than the emergence of new cultural myths, new stories for the collective understanding of *human* experience. This study aims to provide an extended analysis of this newly emergent motion, a gradual "lighting out" toward new territories of being, and of becoming, a hero.

2. Remaking Psyche

Intreat me not to leave thee, or to return from following after thee: for whither thou goest, I will go; and where thou lodgest, I will lodge: thy people shall be my people, and thy God my God:

Where thou diest, will I die, and there will I be buried: the Lord do so to me, and more also, if ought but death part thee and me.

—RUTH 1: 16–17

"The simple act of telling a woman's story from a woman's point of view is a revolutionary act," writes Carol Christ. "It has never been done before."[1] But what female-specific legends, what woman-centered plots, what precursors of the feminized quest-romance have women writers looked toward while envisioning active, courageous heroes? The search for prototypes reveals not so much a scarcity of bold, searching women, but rather a gender teleology that undervalues acts of female heroism by exalting male examples and male experience as definitive. How, for example, would we understand the heroism expressed in Ruth's statement? What are we to make of the words of a widowed daughter-in-law dutifully bound to her mother-in-law?

This much seems clear: Ruth's subversion of patriarchal law requires a new concept of female heroism based on a radical overturning of custom, tradition, and law. No complacent voyager, Ruth becomes a hero at the moment of declaring her own mind and beginning a quest contingent—for the time being—upon relationship with a maternal figure rather than a second husband. Her words of devotion to Naomi suggest a heroism defined by fluid ego boundaries—not a self-sacrificing fluidity, but a strengthening of selfhood derived through, and expressed profoundly in, the act of choosing—rather than passively accepting a companion.

The legend of Psyche presents a prototype for the feminized quest in which the search for enlightened love and for self-knowledge in-form one another in the process of female development. Held captive in the luxurious darkness of Eros's chamber, Psyche's love remains literally blind, dumb, and submissive. Before the act of disobedience provoked by Psyche's sisters, the marriage of Psyche and Eros parallels the state of unconscious bliss that precludes self-knowledge. The sisters, who embody the forces of "sinister wisdom" which precondition women's independent psychic growth, admonish Psyche against her complicity with a husband who, they assure her, is in truth a monster. When at last Psyche breaks her promise to Eros and lifts the lamp to behold his sleeping, youthful face, Psyche, like Eve, satisfies a taste for knowledge and vision which puts an abrupt end to paradisaical, childlike ignorance. Although her act is traditionally read as exemplifying insatiable feminine curiosity, feminist readings admit that there is nothing particularly devilish in Psyche's wanting to know who she is in bed with. Addressing her lover as "light of my life," she is now truly able to "light out" on a quest toward her own spiritual development and her reclamation of a higher love with Eros.

According to Erich Neumann's analysis, Psyche's act results in "the pain of individuation, in which a personality experiences itself in relation to a partner as something other, that is, as not *only* [my emphasis] connected with that partner."[2] My reading, however, locates a more emphatic pain of balancing a dual capacity which remains central to women's quest. For while Psyche's rebellious assertion defines her as the active "hero" of the tale, it is, at last, her ability to love—and to know *herself* in love—which sets her heroism within the context of a complex object-relational structure. This context, like the legend of Psyche itself, challenges the supposition that heroism may be achieved only through the absolute separation of subject and object. Psyche's conflict revolves around a struggle between her desire to be both lover and beloved. This struggle is symbolically expressed in the opposition of love in the dark and love in light. The spatial division of Eros's cave and the world ruled by Aphrodite further underscores the essential duality. The paradox which Psyche must confront in her quest is that in order to know Eros, she must sacrifice him and discover her own strength and her own desire.[3] By enduring rigorous trials at the mercy of archetypal feminine forces and by finally balancing the powers of male and female, or nurturance and autonomy in her own nature, Psyche succeeds in discovering an authentic love, a love which ultimately leads her to worldly transcendence and a home among the immortals.

According to Lee R. Edwards, the goal of Psyche's quest is love and social change. These objects are linked through "a revised sense of the possibilities of individual relationship" and also through the fully realized psychic development of both men and women.[4] The hero who experiences relationships as powerfully as he or she experiences solitude requires a quest based on a new set of patterns, metaphors, and themes. While male quests develop characteristically through the male hero's flight from woman and his resistance to the influence of others, feminized quest plots tend to be more accepting of relationships with both men and women as integral to the female's process of realizing individual goals and fulfilling societal needs. The issues surrounding relationship—merger, separation, attachment, and detachment—contribute fundamentally to moving the woman onward in her personal development. Marriage may represent her goal, as in the traditional nineteenth-century marriage plot, or a stumbling block, particularly in contemporary quests where women are granted greater autonomy and more options for adulthood. Adultery, an act that threatens patriarchal stability no less than the female hero herself, may provide a means to her quest or an end, as in the case of Emma Bovary. Friendship with men and women may occasion mutually enabling quests or instances of unthinkable betrayal, as in the friendship of Nel Wright and Sula Peace. But the wish to remake Psyche in a way so as not to gain heroism at the expense of relationship or gain necessary attachments at the expense of self-realization remains a guiding light in the development of women's quest-romance throughout the nineteenth century and into the late twentieth century, when the feminization of the quest truly emerges.

In "The Hero Today," the final section of *The Hero with a Thousand Faces*, Joseph Campbell qualifies the encompassing purpose of his monomyth to assert that while all quests essentially serve the same cultural and spiritual aims, "the circumstances of local life, race, and tradition must all be compounded in the effective forms." Thus, he concludes, while the symbols of the quest may change according to historical and geographical influences, "it is necessary for men to understand, and be able to see, that through various symbols the same redemption is revealed."[5] However, the feminization of quest-romance considers the possibility that a quester might seek redemption *from* the symbols themselves rather than *through* them. The feminization of the quest is not simply a pattern for discovering alternative symbols for the representation of female power and mobility. Rather, the feminized quest searches out and considers new cognitive strategies—new ways of communicating the questing experience and new ways for thinking and talking about experience.

From the union of Psyche and Eros another hero is born, a daughter named Pleasure. But for all of Psyche's progeny who have dared to embark upon the quest, pleasure, like the language which signifies it, is a double-edged sword. When women reject a female identity prescribed by male images and desires, they do not simply resist a conceptual category but an entire mode of conceptualization, a totalizing framework of male-centered symbols and logic.

The contradictions that women writers have had to confront in remaking an authentic Psyche, and the need for them to claim a place within the heroic tradition while asserting their dissociation from that tradition, have led many women writers to adapt a form predicated on the dynamic interplay of polarities in both the culture and the mind of the individual writer, quest-romance.

In many nineteenth-century precursory engagements of the female quest-romance, the task of the woman protagonist is not drastically to change the world to suit her own needs and aspirations but somehow to resolve two conflicting imperatives: her own desire to become a self-sufficient, self-realized adult and society's demand that she become a woman. In nineteenth-century quests that end with the woman's marriage, resolution entails accepting her social role as wife. Marriage offers her a point of rest, stasis, and implicit closure, however illusory or ambiguous the sense of an ending conveyed. The female protagonist may embrace her passions, she may be granted her adventures, she may endure her trials, but primarily en route to discovering that the quest must ultimately lead her to marriage or a death, for, indeed, what else can a heroine do?

Consequently, the desires of the female protagonist are shaped by her need to fit herself into oppressive patriarchal structures from which she can envision no escape. The results of such conflict are evident in works such as *Jane Eyre*, *Middlemarch*, and Susan Warner's *The Wide Wide World*. In these novels, the pattern of domestic enclosure and escape, which Sandra Gilbert and Susan Gubar have discussed in *The Madwoman in the Attic*, highlights the problem of remaking an authentic female psyche that we find everywhere in nineteenth-century fiction. Rather than opening new territories and creating new alternatives to social convention, the female quester develops in accordance with a society that confines her, reshapes her aspirations, makes her aware of limitations, and leads her to resolve her quest only in socially available terms.

Jane Eyre's resolution of the quest through marriage achieves not so much a balance of opposed forces as a resignation to the demands of the social sphere. The conventional marriage plot ultimately serves patriarchal culture by maintaining its checks and balances. The female quester who seeks completion or refuge through marriage confines herself to an exceedingly limited social destiny. In this sense Jane's famous declaration, "Reader, I married him," may be taken as no personal triumph—no answer to Jane's prayers for freedom—but an abdication of the quest, a compromise of vision (Jane literally becomes Rochester's eyes), and a grateful acceptance of an end to motion, a lasting confinement and subservience to home and husband.

Changing her name to subvert the very title of the book, Jane Eyre becomes Mrs. Rochester, anticipating Carol Christ's qualification of women's quest plots that culminate in an act of renaming. In the case of the marriage plot, however, the woman often does not change her name to subvert oppressive standards but rather weds the very conventions from which she had initially hoped to escape. The marriage plot thus offers a critique of the seemingly inescapable patterns, images, plots, and forms in which female "heroines" are inevitably caught.

Certainly, women's quests that conclude with marriage as the inevitable denouement are not limited to nineteenth-century novels. In twentieth-century plots as well a striking number of female protagonists reach an implicit completion of the quest's cycle through marriage or through childbirth, both often sanctifying the essential spiritual worth of woman's sociobiological destiny. Recent feminist theorists have, of course, reconsidered these typical patterns, challenging the view that anatomy is destiny. Not only do they propose that women's destinies need not be determined by their biology, but, furthermore, that motherhood is less a mystical, natural fulfillment in the course of female development than a cultural implant, a result of social and economic patterns that maintain sharp divisions between gender occupations. Carol Gilligan's key feminist text, *In a Different Voice*, suggests that woman's emphasis on relationship indicates neither a failed nor compromised developmental quest but a different one. Nevertheless, the female quester who sees marriage or motherhood not as an end in itself but as one of *many* possible steps in what is essentially her own psychic development continues to challenge a predominant view of woman as most fulfilled when serving others' needs rather than her own.

Female quests often recount very early on in the hero's development an experience of abandonment, abuse, or injustice that serves in one way to mark the protagonist's call to the quest and to signal her dire need for salvation through the pursuit of heroic destiny. In *Jane Eyre* the alienation that Jane experiences at Gateshead Hall, her entrapment in the Red Room, underscores her heroic possibilities in sentimental terms. However, equally important to our sense of Jane Eyre as a "heroine" locked *in* is our sense of her as a hero courageously, though transiently, locked *out* from the society of "normal" nonheroic females. Orphanhood allows her—as it does so many nineteenth-century female protagonists—to remain an object of sentiment and fascination, while becoming potentially a subject of radical discontinuity, self-possession, and self-creation. Jane's courage and independence—traits necessary for the enactment of the heroic quest—imply furthermore her distance from the usual standards of feminine meekness and dependency. But what makes Jane Eyre particularly compelling as a potential female hero—and, thus, as an outsider to the dominant culture—is that she personifies a threat to patriarchal uniformity. In this sense, all protagonists of female quest plots are, in Edwards's words, "an image of antithesis. . . . an emblem of patriarchal instability and insecurity."[6] The abuse and isolation that so many female protagonists suffer en route to becoming heroes suggests that the feminization of the quest calls for a female hero who will expose the instability of patriarchal institutions and launch a revolution from the margins of social experience.

Two subtle American precursors of the feminized quest are Susan Warner's *The Wide Wide World* (1850) and Maria Susanna Cummins's *The Lamplighter* (1854). Orphaned and thrown out into the

world as young girls, Warner's Ellen and Cummins's Gertrude remain throughout the tumultuous course of their quests equally determined to overcome circumstances through unrelenting humility,
self-sacrifice, and devotion to the values of God and home. Both
have female mentors who act as spiritual guides to their suffering
companions: Alice Humphries encourages Ellen in her Christian
duty and constancy; Emily Graham, although blinded by an accident, exemplifies through her charity and goodness a true vision of
eternal enlightenment for Gertrude. Ultimately both heroines are
rescued from their quests, rewarded for their obedience with husbands who will devote themselves to protecting them from the evils
of the world.

Such novels have evoked mixed reactions from feminist readers.
Even Jane Tompkins—who argues that women's culture and social
status were empowered by the sentimental novels and novelists of
the nineteenth century—admits that the imperative of womanly
duty and meekness "violates everything the feminist movement has
taught women about the need for self-assertion."[7] However, as Nina
Baym accurately points out, quest-romances that taught women to
behave in this manner "do not merely reflect a current ideology of
womanhood; they participate vigorously in constructing and analyz-
ing such an ideology."[8] The fact that these books were received en-
thusiastically by the unliberated women of earlier generations indicates that domestic romances offered female readers a form of secret
rebellion rather than a guidebook to conventionally Victorian female
behavior. Turning away from New England Calvinism, Cummins's
novel demonstrates through its orphaned female protagonist that
even the most powerless of society's victims may strengthen herself
against adversity and become a hero simply by recognizing the powers of enlightenment within."[9] In *The Lamplighter*, Psyche's torch
translates into the goodness of Trueman Flint, the lamplighter who
offers Gertrude shelter and warmth. Gertrude equates the powers of
his kindness with God's powers to light the stars, and eventually she
learns to look for this light within herself when all else fails her.[10] As
Tompkins states, "One cannot run away in the world of nineteenth-
century women's fiction. . . . escape, consequently, is the one thing
their novels never offer. . . . "[11] In this context, "lighting out," as
opposed to *Huckleberry Finn*'s secular and territorial context, be-

comes a metaphor for the greatest freedom that women could hope
for in their circumstances: religious enlightenment, or the hope of
kindling an inner spiritual torch to hold against the darkness.

Imagining a protagonist who is female as well as orphaned, women
writers contrast the male hero's capacity to survive by his wits with
the female hero's capacity to survive according to standards of feminine "goodness" and lack of guile. As Judith Fetterly remarks,
"Even the poorest male gains something from a system in which all
women are at some level his subjects."[12] A poor, orphaned girl, however, has seemingly little to offer the world and even less to gain. An
interesting parallel between nineteenth-century orphans and their
contemporary female descendants exists in the kinds of family ar-
rangements which earlier and more recent texts depict. Like their
typically orphaned predecessors, modern protagonists seem frequently to lack one or both parents. In the texts examined in this
study, such a pattern is evident: Jean Stafford's Molly Fawcett is fa-
therless; Mary McCarthy's parents die of influenza, leaving her and
her brothers orphaned in the hands of spiteful relatives; Anne
Moody's father leaves his wife and children for another woman; in
Housekeeping, Ruth is abandoned by both biological parents, her father long missing, her mother a suicide; in *Anywhere But Here*, Ann
is raised by her mother and grandmother, having lost both her biological father and stepfather in the aftermath of two divorces.

What these more recent familial configurations reveal is a reflection of contemporary social conditions (i.e., divorce rates, single
motherhood) *and* imagined explorations of the psychic bonds that
determine female development in relation to the presence or absence
of one or both parents. The female hero who lacks a mother may
explore woman's lack of authority in the paternal sphere. She may
rediscover maternal history and culture through the course of psychoanalysis, female bonding, or social activism. The absence of a
father may provide an opportunity to reconsider the father's role in
female development. Furthermore, the removal of the father makes
room for the exploration of issues surrounding maternal identification; it becomes not only possible but necessary to focus exclusively
on the impact of the mother-daughter relationship in the quest of the
female hero.

"By the beginning of the twentieth century," observes Edwards, "novelists seem readier to abandon the project of entrapping the female heroic character and begin the task of inventing maneuvers whereby she can break out of familial, sexual, and social bondage into an altered and appropriate world."[13]

While marriage and acceptance of limitations constitute the major developmental tasks of early women's quest-romances, the novels of the late nineteenth and early twentieth century exhibit a somewhat different pattern as denouements of the quest reflect women's altered social status, political objectives, and strategies of expression. Works such as Kate Chopin's *The Awakening*, Charlotte Perkins Gilman's "The Yellow Wallpaper," and Virginia Woolf's *The Voyage Out* record experiences of suicide, madness, and fatal illness as protests against societal restrictions on women's developing minds and bodies. These stories also record a flight into strategic self destruction as women writers struggle to discover an authentic expression of woman's plight in patriarchal society. Death, in this sense, must be understood as no mere gesture of defeat but as a cry for action and an appeal to readers.

When a woman achieves transcendent heroism through suicide or madness, she ends her quest not simply by rejecting life as a woman but by rejecting life as a woman *here* and *now*—in a society that oppresses women. Indeed, in these instances, a very powerful statement is made. However, while the social implications of this statement are dramatic, the price is dear, and it remains a controversial question as to whether such occasions of death and suicide successfully reflect a perceived cultural need for female heroism. Female death quests perpetuate an image of woman as victim; the equation of death and spiritual triumph may certainly be problematic when the question "How does one *live* as a woman?" is seemingly dismissed with this reply: "One dies." Plots that resolve the woman's trials through death *do*, nevertheless, attempt to restore society in the classic manner of the heroic quest by indicating that a transformational rebirth of both woman and community is not only necessary but imminent. Through death, the female hero prepares the way for individual and social transformation; at the same time, she resolves the tension of the narrative by putting the conflict of female protagonist and culture to rest.

Rachel Brownstein has defined the traditional marriage plot as a female protagonist's search for worth through attaining the love of a man: "When, at the end, this is done, she is transformed: her outward shape reflects her inner self, she is a bride. . . ."[14] Contrary to this end, the feminization of quest-romance moves away from marriage toward different goals. A female protagonist may *become* heroic by ending an unhappy or lifeless marriage; her quest may begin from the moment she becomes divorced or widowed. Her awakening to heroic destiny may take the form of a recognition that she needs to leave her family and children behind in order to make time for herself, to be alone for a while. The feminization of the quest does not describe the process by which women are molded to fit expected patterns, but rather attempts to transform patterns to make them more appropriate and compatible with developing female psyches. Thus the feminized form searches for what is true to women's experience and seeks to invest new myths, forms, patterns, and strategies with this authenticity.

The feminist psychoanalytic theorist Jessica Benjamin writes, "Finding woman's desire . . . requires finding an alternative to phallic structures, to the symbolic mode. And that means an *alternative mode of structuring the psyche, not just a symbol to replace the phallus*." According to Benjamin, an authentic sense of self may be expressed for women through "intersubjectivity," an alternative to the symbolic mode that privileges phallic structures as representations of power, selfhood, and desire. A revolutionary psychic mode, intersubjectivity "refers to what happens between individuals, and within the individual-with-others. . . ." Benjamin further suggests, "The intersubjective mode assumes the possibility of a context with others in which desire is constituted for the self. It thus assumes the paradox that in being with the other, I may experience the most profound sense of self."[15]

Thus, intersubjectivity challenges the coherence of the solitary hero—the staunchly self-sufficient psyche—by expressing and empowering a capacity for self-realization through identification with others. Consequently, such narrative issues as point of view, separation of subject and object, and intrapsychic versus extrapsychic experience may require redefinition. In feminized quests, recognition of others as subjects in their own right and relationships between two equal subjects—woman and man, woman and woman, man and man—are essential to the protagonist's heroic development. In many contemporary women's quest plots, and in the two most recent novels which this study explores, the feminized quest is imagined as a collaborative or intersubjective quest. Heroism is thus defined in a heroic pairing of subjects—for example, Ruth and Sylvie in *Housekeeping*—or in a community of equally independent, yet related subjects, as in the example of the three generations of women who narrate *Anywhere But Here*.

Not to exclude men from this context, intersubjectivity between masculine subjects, as in the case of close male friendship, or "buddy" plots, has come to characterize many recent American portrayals of male heroism, particularly in the realm of popular culture—i.e., Crockett and Tubbs on "Miami Vice" and the characters played by Charles Grodin and Robert DeNiro in the film *Midnight Run* (1988). However, a distinction might be made between such famous male pairs as Huck and Jim, Ishmael and Queequeg, Sal Paradise and Dean Moriarity, Captain Kirk and Mr. Spock, and intersubjective pairings which challenge the very foundation of male bonding as it is culturally constructed.

In the male quest plot, heroic identity tends to be aggressively defined, and friendship, however genuine, expresses itself essentially as a force to counter impending social disintegration. This is especially true in the case of racially or culturally mixed pairings, such as Cooper's Hawkeye and Chingachgook or Twain's Huck and Jim. In these instances, the dark comrade or "other" often constitutes a kind of fantasy for the primary male subject, a projection of an undeveloped or subconsciously repressed aspect of the self. In this sense, as Leslie Fiedler has hypothesized, the "other" represents no subjective presence, but an agent of catharsis that empowers the primary subject. The tendency in American literature to romanticize this pattern indicates a quest toward absolute self-possession and coherent subjectivity through the domination of principles and qualities which the dark comrade serves to personify. Intersubjectivity, however, strives to acknowledge "that the other person really exists in the here and now, not merely in the symbolic dimension."[16] When identity is sustained by the formation of impenetrable ego boundaries, all significant "others" tend to be cast into this symbolic sphere. However, when a subject is able to yield boundaries, when he or she is able to recognize and communicate with an equally responsive and autonomous subject, intersubjectivity opens a path to self-discovery by sustaining—along with separateness—a primary and lasting experience of interconnectedness.

How does authentic female experience become manifest in narrative form? At times, woman's quest may seem to be taking her in circles rather than in a linear direction. She may appear to be moving backward rather than forward, regressing instead of progressing, performing actions out of chronological sequence. For women's narratives, as for women's lives, fragmentation, discontinuity, and digression constitute appropriate means for expressing the female subject, a subject split by a "phallocentric system . . . which defines her as the object, the inessential other. . . ."[17] While it would be an oversimplification to say that the feminized form emphasizes means over ends, process over goals, it is significant to note that the developmental goal of woman's quest *may be to discover and name* its own processes, to locate its proper means. The feminized quest is one acutely aware of and devoted to confronting the problems inherent in its own structuring. The shift in the conditions and denouements of women's quests from the nineteenth to the twentieth century occurs within the context of a shift in narrative possibilities and social conditions that help move the female subject from entrapment to emergence. In an effort to avoid the snares of traditional forms associated with male images, feminized quests often employ the implements of modernist or experimental fiction which emphasize the anarchy of the subconscious and the dislocation of the subject over the assumed stability of socially constructed "reality." Fictional autobiography, fantasy, science fiction, nonlinear discourse, fragments, multiple points of view, or any combination of these may thus constitute the feminized quest's challenge to patriarchally constructed forms.

♋

At a similar moment in my life, too, I went away. I drove off the road I had travelled with my friends and discovered a solitary valley where I dared meet up with an overwhelming emotion. It marked my life with a radical departure. After that walk I would never again be able to take anything for granted about myself or my perceptions of the world.[18]

In *Reinventing Eve: Modern Woman in Search of Herself*, Kim Chernin weaves autobiographical narrative and reflections on culture, myth, and psychoanalytic theory into the account of her quest to reinvent herself. This reinvention was guided by the psychic forces she experienced in her own life and then corroborated with her patients in analysis. For Chernin, the journey began with a period of intense dissatisfaction and depression which she terms "initiation" and which parallels Carol Christ's "experience of nothingness," the first stage of woman's spiritual quest. According to Chernin, woman's call to heroic adventure is characterized by a sense of dislocation, despair, and urgency. These tumultuous emotions make it virtually impossible for her to focus her energies or remain indoors. Recalling how she had been persistently driven away from her desk and outside by a nameless desire, Chernin writes: "I began to admit that I had been drawn out of my house by a wish to disinvent myself as patriarchal female, to give myself back to the nature that was in me, grow profusely, overstep my bounds, step out of the confined plot which I had been assigned, and finally admit, in the most radical possible way, that I as a woman did not exist."[19]

Thus begins Chernin's effort to recreate herself. In her view, the feminized quest hinges on a descent, a journey back into the past, into childhood. Aligning herself with maternal identification theories which seek out radical alternatives to developmental structures that standardize male experience, Chernin's struggle involves a fundamental reclamation of the primal female self who unabashedly needs and craves her mother, who worships the powers of the feminine in a state of pleasurable symbiotic attachment. In order for women to envision themselves as powerful beings, capable of spiritual wholeness and transcendence, Chernin suggests, they first must fall, as Eve fell. "Descent proceeds by way of paradox," she claims. "If we cannot tolerate the desolation of this loss we cannot regain our original knowledge of female power. Our future as women is built upon this paradox and our capacity to resolve it."[20]

"Rule breaking is the first law of knowledge," writes DuPlessis.[21] Woman's self-realization is thus defined as an event proceeding from her refusal to comply with patriarchal law. What Chernin holds to be a possible resolution of the female paradox is woman's quest. In

order to reinvent herself, woman must embark on a journey to abandon the impotent mother and rediscover the Goddess, the embodiment of female power renounced in the moment of turning toward the
father as the living symbol of authority. This supreme feminine
force, like the force of Georgia O'Keeffe's vast, all-encompassing
poppy empowered by its full occupation of the canvas, is a reminder
of the first essential space that we occupy as conscious beings, the
mother's field of vision. And it is this mother's face, "the purpose of
the poem," which "fills the room" (Wallace Stevens), that we all
must eventually reclaim in order to become whole beings.[22]

In sharp opposition to the nostalgic view of the feminized quest as
return to the lost Goddess, postmodern theorists such as Donna Haraway maintain the ideological stance that there is *no* "there" to return to, no way to turn back, no powers to reclaim. "I would rather
be a cyborg than a goddess," Haraway has boldly professed.[23] And I
would suggest that the revolutionary agent in this compelling statement is neither the "cyborg" nor the "goddess" but the "rather" with
which Haraway simultaneously asserts the validity of woman's preference and invites her readers to make a choice as well. Indeed, by
asserting and examining such critical choices, women *do* become
active participants in the drama of cultural transformation; however,
in our haste to encode new myths we must be careful to avoid tossing
out the goddess with the bath water, so to speak. Ultimately Haraway's analysis demonstrates that the goddess will not be put to rest
simply as an idealization of a dichotomized knowledge. Like the
cyborg, She too attends to a tumultuous margin where scientific and
feminist discourse collide; and She continues to serve in the quest
by representing women's collective historical subjectivity in multi-
farious dimensions where feminine agencies converse with the natural activities of the world.

In its implications for future representations of female heroism,
Haraway's definition of a "feminist objectivity" or "situated knowledges" parallels Benjamin's figuration of intersubjective space. Both
concepts counter the presumed unity of the knowing subject with the
understanding that when we speak of cognitive quests and epistemological positions we betray a postmodern insistence on the
pieces of things,[24] a contradictory albeit essential plurality of parts.
Thus, subjectivity is acknowledged as always a shared position; the

so-called "objects" of our inquiry really do participate in an active networking of situated knowledges. And while the intersubjective mode assumes the paradox that "in being with the other I may experience the most profound sense of self," feminist objectivity assumes that in acknowledged partial or limited standpoints we may experience the most objective, the most truthful scientific accounts. Indeed, both Benjamin and Haraway launch these highly metaphorical attacks against phallocentric logic in order to destabilize its privileged "form of one-sided autonomy [which] permeates the Western notion of the individual as thinking subject, as explorer of the world."[25]

The marriage of feminism and cyborg politics promises a unique expression of these cultural manifestos. And significantly, many writers—embracing a world where power is determined more by scientific and technological capacity than by spiritual or mystical forces—look to cybernetics while envisioning a viable feminized quest. Alternative genres such as fantasy and science fiction have offered liberating strategies for the telling of stories inconceivable within other culturally available forms. Charlotte Perkins Gilman's *Herland* and the later fictions of Doris Lessing, Dorothy Bryant, Mary Staton, Anne McCaffrey, Ursula K. Le Guin, and Joanna Russ assimilate elements of traditional quest plots into works of cognitive estrangement. And by fragmenting the very forms through which the unity of the subject was sought, feminist science and cybernetic fictions propose a new breed of hero, a "hero which is not one," or a polymorphous fusion of mechanical parts, intersubjective perspectives, and pluralistic modes of knowledge.

Joanna Russ's novel *The Female Man* remains in this sense a central text. The legitimacy of local, partial cognitive positionings is asserted in this feminist reconstitution of the heroic quest. In a manner that anticipates Baudrillard's vision of the private sphere, Russ represents the hero as a communications network, an interplanetary system of partial perspectives from claimed locations. All sites of information (narration) are embodied, but the subject remains a multiple subject, a composite self. They are four women from different worlds and times: Joanna, Jael, Janet, and Jeannine. Here is a hero primed for survival in the postmodern condition, an intersubjective hero in which and through which information is processed by partial translation, differentiation. The eventual meeting of the Four J's, as they are collectively called, involves a journey that is always critical, interpretive, partial, an occasion for power-sensitive ideological positioning.

Women in *The Female Man* achieve heroic status when they are most aware of their differences, and when they are seen in dynamic relation to one another. They are never identical with one another, never quite where they expect one another to be. Rather they are contiguous: their collective narrative is held "within the intimacy of that silent, multiple, diffuse touch," which undermines the authority of phallocentric narrative.[26] Always in touch with itself, the interplanetary hero is similarly neither one nor separate. S/he functions as a vital expression of an epistemological revolution, a moment that has us looking both backward and forward, witnessing simultaneously the feminization of technical multiplicity and cultural nostalgia.

The feminization of the quest is the mythification of the non-isomorphic subject. While reproductive technology and scientific master codes may indicate a longed-for annihilation, rather than demystification, of the feminine, the grass-roots redefinition of female agency portrayed in Russ's novel offers strong evidence in support of technological culture's empowering impact on future narratives involving female heroes who simultaneously remember and dismember myth from innumerable locations. Such narrative strategies may be perceived as radical assaults on our preconceptions of social reality and gender roles.[27] However, we must also admit the cogent, perhaps too literal-minded argument that such fictional modes are politically irresponsible insofar as they assume a kind of social recalcitrance, a refusal to participate in an immediate material reality. But it must also be understood that the initial development of the hero on the verge of her quest is guided by precisely this refusal to accept or work within a perceived dominant system. Thus, genre may function for the woman writer as technological or cognitive estrangement functions for the protagonist (and the reader) of future quests: the female's heroic quest, incompatible with current social reality, finds its expression in a form structurally detached from current time, place, and any dominant perception of the "real."

That the remaking of Psyche has become a process of popular culture's imagining of women is evident not only in contemporary literature by women, but in the wealth of popular films released since the
mid-seventies—films by both male and female directors—that show
women breaking away from conventional roles and actively engaging
in independent searches for selfhood. Ellen Burstyn's memorable
portrayal of Alice in Martin Scorcese's *Alice Doesn't Live Here Anymore* (1975) feminized the heroic role within the context of a thirty-
five-year-old widow's discovery of self through the trials of reloca-
tion, single-motherhood, and harsh economic reality. More recently,
the adventures of a bored New Jersey housewife in Susan Seidelman's
Desperately Seeking Susan (1985) comprise a comic picaresque
example of the feminized quest for identity. In the dollar-grossing
action/adventure genre, heroes such as Sigourney Weaver's Officer
Ripley, in James Cameron's sequel *Aliens* (1986), suggest a new image of female action and strength that balances Rambolike ven-
geance, futuristic technology, and scientific know-how with maternal
nurturance, receptive ego boundaries, and a self-controlled capacity
for trust. Jane, the intensely focused and creative network news
producer played by Holly Hunter in James Brooks's *Broadcast News*
(1987) and Tess, the ambitious secretary played by Melanie Griffith
in Mike Nichols's *Working Girl* (1988), are female heroes who are
indeed the subjects of their drives, both professional and sexual.
The enormous success of female "buddy" films such as Arthur
Hiller's *Outrageous Fortune* (1987) and television series such as
"Cagney and Lacey" and "Kate and Allie" indicates that the social
need for representations of mutual heroism is occurring alongside
the shift in cultural consciousness that requires fully developed female and male psyches.

The remaking of Psyche is by no means limited to the American
film industry. In *Virgin Machine*, the West German film director
Monika Treut presents a "coming-out" journey that follows Dorothy,
a journalist conducting research on romantic love, from Germany to
San Francisco's lesbian community. When she falls in love with a
male impersonator, what Dorothy begins to discover is the essence of
"true love" with neither a woman nor a man, but in an expression of
her own desire to love and discover a dual capacity in her own nature. In the French film *Vagabond*, Agnes Varda's far less optimistic
study of female transience, an uprooted, nameless young woman's

path toward self-creation brings her into brief contact with others who attempt in some way to mold her, although she will not be molded. Her unexplained death at the conclusion of the film is disturbing, not so much because of any moral overtones conveyed, but precisely because it is unexplained. Consequently, we are defied in our desire to *know* her death, just as the desires of the other characters to know the vagabond are defied by her transience. Finally, her life and her death remain certain in only one sense: they belonged to no one but herself.

Psyche begins her quest with a lamp that she lights in order to see her captor and know enlightened love, a love of which she is both subject and object. Psyche *chooses* knowledge, not to renounce Eros's affections, but to discover her own desire. However, by igniting her lamp and "lighting out" for this territory, Psyche sacrifices her illusion of eternal stasis and protection; she burns her lover but is ironically "burned" at love herself. And like all burned lovers, she must go once again in search of desire to discover its true source of power within herself.

"Lighting out" is thus an enterprise for romantics and for visionaries, for goddesses and cyborgs. "Lighting out," one gives birth to new possibilities for both self and world. In *Light in August*, the image of Lena Grove lighting out toward Doanes Mill, searching, with child, suggests a world on the brink of a revolution, a departure from the old life to the new. When a female hero undertakes the quest and explores the unknown realm of the female psyche, she holds up a lamp to confront the shadows of the past. When modern woman remakes Psyche, she lifts her lamp to see that there remain a thousand more faces to be studied before the quest can be claimed equally by all who look from darkness into light.

"Remember," the Female Man tells us, "I didn't want and don't want to be a 'feminine' version or a diluted version or a special version or a subsidiary version or an ancillary version, or an adaptable version of the heroes I admire. I want to be the heroes themselves."[28] This is not the death of the subject. It is the exhortation of the situated self. But to make her situation heroic, our multiple desires must be claimed as part of a shared mythology that is both confrontational and accountable, caught up in a moment of history that is both humanizing and dehumanizing. In the following chapter, we shall examine the harsh sanction of the latter.

3. Remembering Molly

Jean Stafford's
The Mountain Lion

This is the day when no man living may 'scape away.
—STAFFORD, AUTHOR'S NOTE, *THE MOUNTAIN LION*

As a student at the University of Colorado, Jean Stafford spoke these words in a production of *Everyman*. She played Good Deeds, and years later, while preparing an Author's Note for a reprint of her novel *The Mountain Lion*, she speculated on why she—a female—had been chosen to play a male part: "I suppose it could be argued that out there, in those olden, golden days, we were already on to the treacheries deriving from Male Chauvinism, and this was a little bitty protest. I think it is more likely, however, that I spoke his lines because I had (and have) the voice of an undertaker." [1]

It is significant that Stafford should remark casually on the "treacheries" of sexual prejudice while lamenting the end of her rebellious young protagonist, Molly Fawcett. Like the young Stafford, Molly realized at an early age the unlikelihood of a woman's plot to deconstruct gender. And also like Stafford, Molly participated, however unwittingly, in an uncertain act of rebellion. *The Mountain Lion* constitutes Stafford's own "little bitty protest" against cultural and literary codes that give women the option of either remaining backstage or disguising their female identity in order to surreptitiously assume a masculine part.

The words of Good Deeds provide a fitting backdrop for understanding the problematic validity of *The Mountain Lion* as a feminist text. Blanche Gelfant has rightly observed that this powerful novel "belongs to the wasteland tradition of apocalyptic writing. . . ." [2] And while the timeless quality of the novel remains undisputed, its unique revelation of doom reflects the workings of a modern imagination specifically attuned to the fundamental yet fatal trappings of the American literary tradition for the woman writer. Although earlier readings tended not to focus on the problem of gender difference, many recent feminist critics have been strikingly alert to the subtle strategies with which Stafford mocks the sexual policing of the Great Frontier of American legend and lore.

Stafford's pronouncement of apocalypse does not fall generally upon Everyman or Everywoman, but upon one unlikely adolescent misfit whose vision of salvation (she wants to grow up to become a writer) is no match for the cultural forces conspiring to limit her aspirations and deprive her of autonomy. And indeed it is this apocalyptic awakening to immobility and impotence, a violent transformation of mythical potential into disdainfully naturalistic ruin, a rechanneling of romantic forms through an acutely ironic vision, that has, according to Ihab Hassan, made it possible to define the contemporary American novel as "a parody of man's quest for fulfillment," a thwarted journey which tends to culminate "either in the isolation of the hero or in his defeat," thus turning the post-1945 novel into "a study of self-deception."[3] The "heroes" of these adventures are new-fangled questers in search of a "radical innocence," descendants from Cooper, Melville, Twain, and James in the longstanding tradition of quest-romance.

Hassan's thesis affirms Stafford's participation in this tradition by illuminating evidence of her estrangement from it. The conflict with tradition, the father's law, remains the sine qua non of paradoxical logic regarding the "great" American authors, texts, and themes. The very essence of the American novel evolved from this struggle, "the perception and acceptance . . . of radical disunities."[4] Yet this kind of theorizing also assumes the logic of Oedipal politics, a logic that bolsters the image of struggling sons and envious daughters. Consequently, and not surprisingly, of Stafford's three novels *The Mountain Lion* (1947) is the most highly acclaimed by Hassan and other critics who emphasize Stafford's reliance on the ironic mode as well as her contradictory stance in relation to the conventional forms and themes of American fiction. I will argue, however, that *The Mountain Lion* should not be remembered for engaging the keynote conflict, but for exploiting it in an effort to transform the literary "heroine" into a female hero, and the quest-romance into an endangered species.

Remembering *The Mountain Lion* requires that we respond to, and to some degree resist, the difficulty presented by the novel's ending. Certainly, readers may never know how much of an emotional investment they have in hypermasculine American myth until the shocking final pages of the novel. Darkly allusive as the narrative voice remains, Stafford's irony, acidity, rage, and vision converge most ominously when Molly is "accidently" shot to death by her brother, Ralph, while he is out hunting the wild animal of the title. The ending of the novel occasions some brutal assumptions about gender and the quest, and it raises some necessary questions: What are the implications of Hassan's "radical innocence" when the hero is female and her holy grail is freedom from the bleak reality of gender restrictions? What are the longings of the "refractory soul" whose social status and aspirations are limited because of its confinement in the female body? Must the cultural contradictions reflected in literary form be interpreted differently when the writer is a woman and her subject is woman at odds with inner strengths and desires judged inappropriate by society?

Provisional responses are inadequate; however, feminist and nonfeminist critics agree that while the collective assessment of our traditional canon seems relentless in its discernment of forces always at odds, these oppositions signify, in the case of the woman writer, a vital and dynamic relationship to her culture's standards for feminine character. Furthermore, these oppositions will reflect, in her work, a capacity for self-realization and survival under these conditions. Therefore, even though Jean Stafford's work may support general critical claims regarding the cataclysmic implications of our American identity crisis, her vision remains, and must be understood as, a product of gendered experience. And while Stafford, in the unprolific latter part of her career, outspokenly opposed the popular platform of women's liberation, her novels and short stories engage the central issues and contradictions that motivated the growth of women's literature in the United States. Chief among the concerns addressed in her fiction are the fears and disappointments of childhood, the plight of female adolescence in a culture that exalts and romanticizes male youth, and the fraudulence and warped values of the adult world.

The Mountain Lion touches upon all of these themes, although it answers to none of them; Stafford's achievement is in articulating and pointing out the destructive power they have for the female imagination. What is realized throughout the development of the narrative is literally a dead end, a lack of any viable territory for a female initiation into mature, independent adulthood. And what emerges in the tragic conclusion of the novel is the need for a radical departure from the literary forms, social conventions, and rituals of initiation that operate by men, for men, through the annihilation of the female. In *The Mountain Lion*, we see the feminization of the American quest-romance at the threshold of its realization.

The settings Stafford chose for her fictions span from Europe to Boston to California, but the landscape she seemed most to prefer was the American West during its time of rapid transformation and modernization. This was the part of the country that Stafford herself experienced while growing up in rural California and rocky Colorado, landscapes that would both find their way into *The Mountain Lion*. While Stuart Burns sees this setting as a backdrop for "a saga of a changing America,"[5] Melody Graulich's insightful analysis of *The Mountain Lion* explains Stafford's adoption of the American Western theme as a way of exposing, specifically, the "destruction of the feminine." According to Graulich, Stafford, by placing her novel within the prototypical landscape of masculine fantasy, is able to address "her struggles as a woman writer using male conventions and writing within a male tradition."[6] Earlier, Blanche Gelfant, in an important essay discerning "an uncertain tension within [*The Mountain Lion*] between form and theme," defines the main action of the novel as "an overturning of expectations: a subversion of forms, myths, and manners which it draws on only to demolish."[7] From a feminist viewpoint, however, Stafford's novel does much more than respond to the loss of childish innocence, a symbol of our treasured, albeit illusory American myths. Although the novel reiterates the familiar themes of innocence versus experience, East versus West, reality versus romance, and nature versus civilization, these tensions serve chiefly to underscore what I see as Stafford's primary objective: to expose the traditional questing theme's dependence on the death, or mastery of, the feminine.

The Mountain Lion tells the story of Ralph and Molly Fawcett, ages ten and eight respectively. As the narrative opens, the siblings' attachments to childhood fantasies—and to one another—are shattered by the death of their grandfather and by the initial stirring of Ralph's adolescent self-awakening. The Fawcett children live in a

quiet section of suburban California with their widowed mother and
their two elder sisters, Leah and Rachel. Impeccably poised, pol-
ished, and socially affected, neither Mrs. Fawcett nor her two older
daughters resemble Ralph and Molly in the least. Sickly and dirty-
looking, socially awkward and intellectually precocious, Ralph and
Molly share an affinity which precludes all adult knowledge and
manners. Rebels both at home and at school, Ralph and Molly take
great mutual pleasure in their defiant behavior and in their spontaneous nosebleeds, which—much to the amazement of their teachers—they always manage to suffer at precisely the same instant.
While Mrs. Fawcett dotes on Leah and Rachel, who know how to use
their sophisticated manners to charm guests, such as the stuffy Reverend and Mrs. Follansbee, Ralph and Molly wage combat with their
innocence; when the neighbors' children speak knowingly about sexual intercourse, Ralph and Molly refuse to listen and promptly beat
them up.

However, as the story develops, Ralph and Molly's relationship
changes. Ralph is no longer so keen on having Molly as his sole con-
fidant. Her intellectual aspirations and the odd pieces of poetry she
insists on reading aloud lead Ralph to the conclusion that his sister
is going crazy. He takes comfort in anticipating the yearly visit from
Grandfather Kenyon, a tough old cattle-ranch tycoon. This year
Ralph hopes to establish some genuine man-to-man contact with his
grandfather, without Molly's interference.

Mrs. Fawcett tolerates her stepfather's visits for the sake of appearances, but she cherishes the memory of her real father, Grandfather Bonney, whose ashes she keeps in an urn on the mantlepiece.
The Bonneys from back east represent all that the Kenyons do not:
civility, worldliness, class, and good breeding. Although she encourages Ralph to follow in the footsteps of the Bonney patriarch,
both he and Molly idolize their Grandfather Kenyon, whom they
think of as glamorous, authentic, and just a little bit dangerous.

The Fawcett household receives a shock when, during his visit,
Kenyon dies suddenly of a heart attack. When his son, Claude, arrives from Colorado, Ralph is especially surprised to find him simply
a younger version of his grandfather, a real cowboy. To Ralph, Uncle
Claude is a man's man, a spiritual guide to lead him through the
trials on his quest to manhood. In Claude's company Ralph feels

privileged to discover the uncomplicated gestures and expressions of male bonding. It is Claude who first suggests that Ralph and Molly come spend summer on the ranch in the Colorado mountains. And, finally, it is Claude who invites Ralph to participate in the hunt to kill the mountain lion. Thus, when Mrs. Fawcett agrees that a summer in the great outdoors might, in fact, do the children's health some good, Ralph and Molly become candidates in a world of ritual initiation through the quest.

Ralph and Molly's two consecutive summers and their subsequent full year of residence at the Bar K Ranch structure the narrative development of the novel. For Ralph, these summers provide an opportunity to test his manhood, to prove his worth both to himself and to his Uncle Claude, and finally to transcend his initial identification with the Bar K men as he comes to recognize the infantile and egotistical nature of their camaraderie. For Molly, however, the rough surroundings and crude predominance of Uncle Claude and his men offer no model, no guidance for social integration, and no support for developing her creative and intellectual interests. Unlike Ralph, her experience is best described as "an awakening to limitation," a suffocating encounter with the reality of what it means to grow up handicapped by gender.[8]

As Molly and Ralph approach puberty, their capacities for successful growth into adulthood are compared and ultimately determined by family-imposed gender expectations. While Ralph's confidence and initiative are reinforced by social convention, tradition, and the existence of male role models willing to guide him, Molly's adolescent self-awakening is thwarted by her entrapment in male-dominant surroundings and by the lack of a female mentor to show her alternatives to a future of subservience and inferiority.[9] For Molly, no social or spiritual quest nor any hopes for an authentic growth to womanhood exist. And while she ultimately rejects tomboyism, a mere imitation of the male patterns of development, she finds that her efforts to remain true to her own impulses render her a social outcast.

Throughout their childhoods, Ralph and Molly remain one another's sole supports. Yet while Ralph begins to experience an individual sense of worth, Molly's attachment to him is intensified by the lack of a viable female role model. Ralph begins to perceive Molly's

adoration as a threat to his increasing need for independence and
male bonding. Although he cares for Molly, he decides that the one
thing he cannot stand about her is the way she imitates him:

> It was natural for her to want to be a boy (who *wouldn't!*) but he
> knew for a fact she couldn't be. Last week he had had to speak
> sharply to her about wearing one of his outgrown Boy Scout
> shirts: he was glad enough for her to have it, but she had not
> taken the "Be Prepared" thing off the pocket and he had to come
> out and say brutally, "Having that on a girl is like dragging the
> American flag in the dirt." (P. 30)

By imitating Ralph, Molly stands to gain neither "preparedness"
for her own quest nor the privilege of representing American heroic
ideals. While the institution of "scouting" supports the masculine
American rite of "lighting out," Molly is denied the quester's outfit
and is excluded from its symbolic conventions. Even though she
longs to keep her emotional lifeline to Ralph intact, Molly neither
imitates masculine behavior nor longs to become a boy instead of
who and what she is. As her refusal to adopt a "proper" feminine
role becomes pronounced, she is driven not toward an annihilation
of the female but rather toward an intense self-awareness that corresponds to her recognition that she is different from both men and
other women. While this awareness strengthens Molly's individualism, it adds to her sense of isolation and suggests that while females lack their own ennobling badges and mottoes of preparedness
for the quest, their salvation does not lie in the adoption of male
guises but in the search for new, authentic images of scouting the
female psyche.

An incident which has heretofore been unnoticed by critics provides an interesting parallel to the Boy Scout passage. Shortly after
Uncle Claude's arrival at the Fawcett's home, Ralph escapes Molly's
company so that he and his uncle can talk man to man. Much to
Ralph's distress, however, Claude remains impassive toward Ralph's
obvious appeal for masculine approval. And although it is Molly who
holds the family reputation for storytelling, Ralph determines to get
Claude's attention by recounting an episode in which he once ate a
mouthful of nitrate fertilizer, mistaking it for brown sugar. Claude
breaks into laughter; Ralph's narrative strategy signals the begin-

ning of friendship between him and his uncle. And as much as this pleases Ralph, he begins to feel "a little disquieted because [the nitrate incident] had happened to Molly, not to himself" (p. 81).

What we are able to infer from these examples is useful: when Molly imitates Ralph, she does so because she longs to merge with him, to be closer to him; her imitation is a bid for inclusion. When Ralph imitates Molly, however, he does so in order to steal her "life" and thereby to separate from her. But Ralph can only individuate from Molly by appropriating her experience and by absorbing it into his own. The initial gesture of his passage into masculine society is therefore predicated on his exploitation of Molly and his concealment of her ability to assert effective narrative control. Consequently, the more Molly appears to be a character chiefly in relation to Ralph, the more she comes to occupy the center of the novel's consciousness. And those critics who read Molly's function in the novel as chiefly that of obstacle to the fulfillment of Ralph's quest-initiation are arguably in collusion with his act of thievery.

Molly, much like the female reader of American fiction whom Judith Fetterly has described, is thus "co-opted into participation in an experience from which she is explicitly excluded. . . ."[10] And her quest, like the critical quest Fetterly initiates, is to become a "resisting" participant in the male culture which defines itself against her. And from a feminist perspective, this much is clear: although most of *The Mountain Lion* is narrated from Ralph's point of view, the novel belongs to Molly. Her resistance to a culturally defined womanhood informs the direction and the sensibility of the narrative; her presence forms the pattern of Ralph's conscious and unconscious desires to make her vanish. His story remains essentially a story in dialectic relation to Molly's; the more we see through Ralph's eyes, the more we understand and are made aware of Molly. And the more Ralph longs to escape her, the more we realize the futility of his longing. Ralph's perceived "difference" from Molly is, and will eternally remain, that condition by which he defines himself.

In *The Mountain Lion*, Stafford undertakes a critical examination of the literary forms that deny female agency, autonomy, and self-realization through a subversion of the quest motif. And dialectically engaged with these literary forms are the cultural codes that inhibit women's mobility. Stafford's final conclusion—that the day has come for a radical transformation of both the literary and the cultural codes, a transformation founded on the reincarnation of the female protagonist—is developed through an analogue of images and metaphors reflecting Molly's condition of physical and spiritual entrapment in spaces and patterns imminently destructive to her character.

Stafford subverts typical associations between physical spaciousness and imaginative freedom in order to demonstrate Molly's confinement in what Joanne Frye has termed the male-dominant "femininity text."[11] Melody Graulich sees Stafford's use of spatial references as a way of transforming the American theme of the open frontier into a gender-specific reflection on male power and female dispossession. By misinterpreting the lyrics of "America" as "O Beautiful for Spacious Guys," Ralph admits his confidence that, as a boy, America is his (p. 32). Not only does he possess the territory, but the fact of his being male equates him with this spacious expanse. To be male is, indeed, to embody the symbol of the American flag; and when Ralph berates Molly for dragging the flag through the dirt, he accuses her of corrupting the very text of masculine superiority. Graulich confirms that while Ralph's "future is 'spacious' . . . Molly finds her horizon contracting."[12] Like the ladybugs Molly collects and keeps within match boxes, she is socially boxed in by a future limited to fulfilling the needs of others instead of searching for her own fulfillment.

Molly remains, for the most part, a stationary creature. Even in the wide open spaces of the western frontier, the area that Molly occupies seems to shrink, while Ralph's territory expands and widens with each new experience and encounter with the masculine world surrounding him. Molly's inability to enact the necessary motions toward adulthood is emphasized by Stafford's concern with the actual limits of external spaces, her frequent references and images of enclosure. When Molly and Ralph behave rudely to the Reverend Follansbee, Ralph is verbally reprimanded while Molly is physically confined; she is told to have the maid, another confined woman, lock her in the closet. At the Bar K—a name which in itself conveys exclusion, a literal barring from the male elite—Uncle Claude is disgusted with her inertia and makes fun of her for remaining on a bench while the others go horseback riding. Molly's life becomes more and more an inverted quest to take up as little space as possible. Even her own private place in the mountains where she goes to write stories is described as "very small and surrounded so densely

by trees and chokeberry that they were almost like walls . . ."
(p. 206).

Stafford's subversion of the American quest-romance betrays the
influence of one of her favorite writers, Henry James. Exploiting the
"innocents abroad" theme, Stafford reminds readers of the forgotten,
unsung American heroine who never left the shore; quite unlike Is-
abel Archer and Maggie Verver, Molly is not granted the opportunity
to discover America by abandoning it. Thus, when Mrs. Fawcett an-
nounces her intentions of taking Leah and Rachel on a year-long trip
around the world, Stafford's irony is most sharply evident. For Molly,
we recognize, such a trip might have been her salvation, the chance
to discover alternatives to her stifling background and culture. The
experience of travel might have set her mind and spirit in motion
while enriching her professional aspirations to become a writer.

Leah and Rachel, as Molly is fated to learn, could not care less
about the tour. When a letter from Leah reveals that her recent engagement to a boy back east is the motivating factor behind the sudden trip, Molly is nauseated. Not only does Leah's pending marriage
disgust her, but also her blunt disenchantment with having "to go
around the darned old world" (p. 147). Sensitive to the injustice that
Leah's "old world" could have been her new world, Molly's only de-
fense is to take offense. Rejecting the entire matter with a favorite
new word, "bourgeois," Molly renounces "Leah's letter, Leah herself, and the trip around the world" with cold finality (p. 148).

Passively accepting their roles as objects on the marriage market,
Leah and Rachel recall their biblical namesakes, the daughters of
Laban, who become the objects of exchange between their father and
their eventual common husband, Jacob. Molly, too, senses that she
is trapped in a vast system of value and exchange, authority over
which resides primarily in the male domain. However, Molly resists
becoming a commodity to be haggled over and fought for by men. It
is clear that she has no interest in "society," nor in the pursuit of
marriage or wealth. Much to Molly's disgust, her only probable female ally, Winifred Brotherman, finally admits that she takes more
pride in her popularity with boys than in her ability to translate difficult Latin texts into English. Living up to the patriarchal expectation
that women remain emotionally childish and financially dependent,
Winifred, Leah, and Rachel become, in Molly's eyes, "unforgivables." As Ralph begins developing an interest in sex, his name, too,

is added to Molly's list of "unforgivables." And although Ralph is
left behind with Molly when Leah and Rachel go around the world,
his future quests are suggested symbolically. By bestowing upon
Ralph the miniature silver globe that becomes his most valued possession, Grandpa Kenyon clearly spells out the novel's message:
men, not women, may come to possess the world and hold its power
in their hands.

The damaging force of this message is further evinced in Molly's
increasing dread at the fleshly reality of her female body. She tries
very hard to imagine herself as nothing but "a long wooden box with
a mind inside" (p. 177). Her repulsion and fear become manifest in
body-negation and blatantly anorectic behavior. She binds her stom-
ach tightly at night with a piece of flannel and imagines herself "getting thinner and thinner" until she becomes "practically famous for
it" (p. 181). In the act of starvation Molly envisions a triumph of personal and spiritual will over biological and cultural destiny. Molly's
obsession with enclosures and body image are symptomatic of the
anorexia-agoraphobia patterns which Sandra Gilbert and Susan Gubar
have identified as symbolic of women's textual and imaginative entrapment. Molly decides that if she ever got fat "she would lock herself in a bathroom and stay there until she died" (p. 180). Meals, she
imagines, could be hoisted up through the window in a basket on a
rope. Stafford's humorous rendering of Molly's extreme solution to
the body-mind schism is overshadowed by the self-destructive fixation on body function and controlled spaces, a fixation which translates into the enclosure-escape pattern of the text.

Further reinforcing this pattern, Molly creates a universe that she
divides into two parts: herself and the "unforgivables." People's
names may be added to the list of "unforgivables" if they become
"fat" or if they say "fat" things. When, on the train headed west,
Ralph asks Molly to tell him all the dirty words she knows, he, too,
becomes "fat" in Molly's eyes, and she vows to have no more to do
with him. To become "fat," for a man, is to submit to sexual nature.
For women, it means submitting to sexual passivity and domination
by men. Rather than accept this fate, Molly vows never to become
fat. This fierce rejection of sexuality in general, and her own body
in particular, should not, according to Barbara White, be mistaken
for immaturity or Victorian prudery. "It is probably not the act of
sex itself which repulses Molly," White explains, "but the fact that

it reminds her of her inferior role."[13] Thus, Carol Christ defines Molly's situation when she characterizes the essential first step in the schema of women's spiritual quest, the experience of nothingness: "Internalizing the voice of her oppressors, the currents of [Molly's] feelings of inferiority and self-hatred run deep."[14]

The terrible pain that women suffer for their looks is a theme that occurs frequently in Jean Stafford's novels and short stories. In *The Mountain Lion*, Molly's physical ungainliness serves to stress the fact that her development is—in the literal and figurative sense—not a pretty picture in the eyes of society. Molly's ugliness becomes even more isolating as Ralph, whom she so strongly resembles, grows to accommodate his features; he becomes handsome as he matures. But Molly, as she stands before a mirror in a hotel lobby, regards her reflection and remarks to passersby, "Go on, admit I'm prettier than Mary Pickford" (p. 144). Even though her poor posture and dark, inelegant features intensify both her sarcasm and the indifference with which others regard her, Molly demonstrates an admirable degree of strength in her ability to defend herself against the insensitivity of others. It is not, finally, Molly's own disgust with her appearance but her fear of rejection that contributes to the comfort she finds increasingly in antisocial behavior and spiritual withdrawal.

As Molly sees fewer and fewer possibilities for self-realized growth, she detaches more and more from her surroundings and retreats into her own fantasy world. While her visions approximate, to some extent, the self-negation stage of Christ's quest pattern, Molly remains too much in tune with her own desires and her own vision of the world to abandon herself completely to despair. In a real sense, this is Molly's tragedy; psychologically, she remains too sound to survive her oppressive environment. When, finally, Molly adds her own name to the list of "unforgivables," she makes a dramatic bid for inclusion in the world, but, simultaneously, she names herself the very agent of her subversion. Contrary to the new-naming experience which, according to Christ's schema, succeeds self-negation, Molly's is self-named "unforgivable." She encodes herself in the "femininity text" and becomes an embodiment of contradictions she can neither suppress nor accept.

As Molly's quest is inverted, Ralph's sense of power increases as he begins to adapt to life at the ranch: he realizes in male adulthood the privileges of mobility, agency, and autonomy; he becomes comfortable with the processes of maturation and sexuality. His quest to prove his masculine worth to Claude involves him immediately in the traditional rites of passage which affirm male superiority. From Claude, he derives the essential support of a spiritual guide. With Winifred Brotherman, he experiences his first crush. Witnessing the breeding of cattle, Ralph connects male sexual belligerence with the natural order. He begins to take strange delight in seeing "his mother and sisters receive libidinous stares" from strange men, for "while he feels some guilt, he likes the fact of women being prey." [15] When Claude suggests that Ralph's eyeglasses make him look weak, he stops wearing them even though he suffers from headaches and nausea. Traditionally, the hero is required to undertake such difficult tasks in order to achieve the quest's fulfillment. In this sense, Ralph demonstrates his courage to endure suffering. However, in the context of his increasing rejection of Molly and in view of his eagerness to be admitted into the patriarchal order, Ralph's sacrifice symbolizes his adamant rejection of a necessary part of himself, the feminine. As the removal of the eyeglasses suggests, his initiation will require a self-imposed distortion, a deficient vision of the world. As Ralph discerns the need for escaping the female part of himself, he comes to view the feminine as the enemy, that which must be fenced in, forced into submission, or destroyed.

The masculine fear of the female who resists submission and passive imprisonment is represented in the hunt for the mountain lion, the symbol of undomesticated femininity. Enacting the ritual of the hunt, Ralph performs the task most essential to his fulfillment of the quest. By offering Ralph exclusive rights to help him kill the mountain lion, Claude offers the "ultimate boon," the "life-transmuting trophy," which Joseph Campbell sees as essential if the hero is ever to become fully initiated into his society. In *The Mountain Lion*, the society Ralph serves is male society. The service he provides through his fulfillment of the quest is the empowerment and renewal of male supremacy.

Uncle Claude names the lion Goldilocks because her blond, shiny coat makes her look "like a movie star." The connection to Hollywood actresses is significant as an allusion to the roles women are induced to play for men: Mother (Ralph fantasizes shooting the lion with her cubs), Holy Virgin, Sex Goddess, Long-Suffering Wife, Castrating Bitch. Stalking the mountain lion, Ralph stalks the male power to invent the feminine and promote an illusion of femininity. In *The Feminine Mystique*, written some fifteen years later, Betty Friedan would identify this illusion: "[The feminine mystique] says . . . femininity is so mysterious and intuitive, so close to the creation and origin or life that *man-made* [my emphasis] science may never be able to understand it. . . . The mistake, says the mystique, the root of women's troubles in the past is that women envied men, women tried to be like men, instead of accepting their own nature. . . ."[16]

Hoping to kill the mountain lion, Ralph seeks to conquer the female who resists the man-made image, "the devil inside the heroine herself, the dream of [female] independence, the discontent of spirit, and even the feeling of a separate identity. . . ."[17]

That Molly's quest is thwarted should seem horribly tragic to readers because of the hope and expectations that she is able to inspire, even despite the difficult obstacles she confronts. Molly's public appeals for a typewriter are turned down. Her contribution to the state agricultural college, hundreds of ladybugs which she collects from under rocks, goes unacknowledged. Her gift of the feminine insects ignored, her request for the most basic tools denied, Molly is able to elicit no encouragement or validation from the world around her. Nevertheless, it is of crucial significance to our understanding of the novel that Molly continues, in spite of all obstacles, to enact gestures of hope up until the very end. For what promises to make this end difficult for both male and female readers to accept, finally, is not the tragedy of Molly's decline but rather the strength she manages to maintain.

Molly's humorous letters to the president and state officials requesting a typewriter are moving because they show her last-ditch appeal to enlist help from the outside world. In this way, she retains an apparent will to overcome limitations and fulfill her hopes of becoming a writer, her own woman. Although ultimately Molly's brains win her no scholarships, her letters receive no answers, and her objections fall upon deaf ears, what's important is that she *does* think, she *does* write, and she *does* object. Molly recognizes that she is different from other girls, and I believe it shows a triumph of the literary imagination that such a female protagonist makes every effort to insist on this difference up until the very end of her life.

If Molly's end is painful for us it is because we *do* see a future for her. Whether we resist her death or experience relief when she is killed, we do so because on a profound emotional level we understand, as Stafford understood, that Molly was bound for sacrifice. Like Ralph, we cannot consciously acknowledge what deep down we suspect might happen. "Well, I don't know if Molly can come," Ralph says hesitantly when Uncle Claude invites them both to the ranch. "I think maybe something is going to happen to her" (p. 82). The thought both fascinates and unnerves him, just as later in the novel Ralph rationalizes that it is not Claude's but his right to kill the mountain lion because he loves her. "Through killing," writes Gelfant, "as through art, one enters the world of ritual where time is stopped and the past kept intact."[18] As a male, Ralph is the "one" privileged to enter this world. The ritual of the kill echoes the male ritual of the quest as well as the ritual of the text through which time is stopped, images are frozen in language, and objects of love are fixed eternally.

Could it be true, as some critics have suggested, that Molly's shooting was a result of Stafford's failure—her inability—to imagine any kind of future for a rebellious adolescent female? I think not. Rather, I think that Stafford was stuck, fully aware of her predicament, between a rock and a hard place: she could not fulfill, within the conventions and traditions afforded her as an American writer, the promise of Molly's remarkable character without employing the very implements of destruction she hoped to condemn. Consequently, readers may respond less with sympathy for Molly than with anger at having their ending manipulated and their own innocence revealed as equally responsible for Molly's death. Our faith in the transformation of the ugly duckling, in the inevitable victory of the underdog, is violently revealed as the same kind of hokey nonsense that Molly herself would have deplored. In this way, Molly's death exacts a price from readers that some may feel is unfair and aesthetically unsophisticated. Just as Molly pays an enormous price for her individualism, we, as readers, pay for Molly's death with a fortune of faith in the novel's capacity to transcend the obvious.

"Die as a hero; or live as a woman."[19] The possibilities for Molly's future are unfortunately determined—not by Molly herself—but by masculine myth, defending its preeminence at the fringes of extinction. *The Mountain Lion* is a powerful articulation of the central dilemma challenging female identity at a pivotal moment in American women's social and literary development. In Stafford's novel, the feminization of the quest was foreshadowed but ultimately overwhelmed by literary forms and cultural imperatives that impede the motion of women's quests. The paradox of *The Mountain Lion* is that it calls for a feminization of the questing theme through an act of destruction that simultaneously defies the quest's existence while calling it into being. Placed within the context of subsequent female quests, the novel stands today as a resounding protest against women's confinement in small, male-controlled spaces that can no more accommodate the capabilities of their minds than it can the restless longings of their spirits.

Stafford's novel is important for this study, and for feminist critics, because by addressing a problem it began to establish a necessary climate for change. Molly Fawcett did not comply with the world. She did not repress her yearnings. She did not go insane. She neither committed suicide nor did she wither away in the grip of some mysterious, incurable disease. Like the mountain lion, killed in flight, Molly is killed in the special place she dared to call her own, and she is killed, we can assume, while in the act of writing. Thus, she continued to reach out, to forge communication. In her entrapment, Molly symbolized something other than an endangered species: rather, she suggested a new breed of female whose crisis at the transitional age of adolescence suggests a transitional moment in the fight for women's social literary status.

For these reasons, *The Mountain Lion* should be read. And for these reasons, Molly's death should be read as an end presaging a new beginning. Molly died so that she could be reborn again in future female protagonists whose survival, as we shall discover, owes a debt to Molly—a debt which survival itself should compensate for. Although Stafford puts an abrupt end to the growing pains of Molly Fawcett, my sense is that the point of the devastation is to transfer the growing pains to the reader. For it is we who must now come to terms with our literature's annihilation of the female and the end of her development. It is we who must initiate a movement beyond the limits of social expectations. The challenge now is to remember the woman who might have been Molly.

4. "A Kind of Quest"

Mary McCarthy's
Memories of a
Catholic Girlhood

An American armed with the primacy of the self can do anything.
Especially in words. . . . To have a sense of history one must consider
oneself a piece of history. . . . —KAZIN, "THE SELF AS HISTORY"

In these words, Alfred Kazin clearly identifies the dilemma that female autobiographers have faced in their efforts to conceive of women's lives as fundamental and representative pieces of history. The military analogy alone bespeaks the problem: women autobiographers—coming forward to fight their own battles in the field—have, in doing so, overturned masculine territory and patriarchal conditions that would render women's autobiographical acts blatant contradictions in cultural and literary terms. Consequently, just as American women have been excluded from the mostly male chorus intoning its sacred song of self, so have they been denied the armor of qualified selfhood as well as those life experiences with which such protective shields are adorned.

Indeed, American autobiography *is* American history; a fixation on the mechanisms of the self helps define American history, as it helps define what is compelling in American literature. What other nation, what other culture can claim such a time-honored and beloved fascination with self-reliance, the solitary leaf which, only when multiplied, constitutes the entire field of grass? If we regard egocentrism as a national trait, we may regard autobiography as truly the most American of literary genres; from the "Personal Narratives" of Jonathan Edwards to the "Account" of Washington Irving to the "*Advertisements* . . ." of Norman Mailer, the genre of American self-writing emerges as a reflection of a powerful impulse in our national character: to proclaim "I am" and to ask in the same breath, "Who Am I?" asserts individual specialness. Alfred Kazin makes this claim: "The deepest side of being an American is the sense of being like nothing before us in history . . . the experience of being so *much* a 'self'—constantly explaining oneself and telling one's story— is as traditional in the greatest American writing as it is in a bar- room."[1] This tradition of self-explanation, however, like the barroom camaraderie Kazin sanctifies, exalts male-specific experience and affirms male creative power. But beyond the creation of a "manly," independent personal identity, the autobiographical act allows one to participate in the creation of a public and national identity.

"If the act of recreating one's past and discovering one's identity is a riskier enterprise for women than it is for men, that is because such an occasion is likely to challenge traditional beliefs (usually enunciated by men) about what it means to be an American fe- male."[2] Here Albert E. Stone describes the personal dilemma that becomes public when women autobiographers try to assert an au- thentic female self and break with male-sanctioned ideas about fe- male ability and identity. In order to assert this self, women writers have departed from cultural definitions that emphasize women's bio- logical and nurturing capacity, their secondary role in the American legacy. The rugged individualist ideal that has shaped so much male autobiography and fiction traditionally accords women a part that matters only in relation to men, roles such as devoted daughter, sis- ter, wife, mother. According to Stone, these "familiar formulations" of womanhood "function both as myth and as ideology, for each as- serts as timeless fact something which serves the immediate interest of particular groups, conspicuously men."[3] What little precedent was set for the formulation of the female subject through autobio- graphical works by such widely known women as Helen Keller, Elizabeth Cady Stanton, Margaret Mead, Gertrude Stein, Anaïs Nin, Charlotte Perkins Gilman, Ida B. Wells, Isadora Duncan, Eleanor Roosevelt, and others has remained complicated and obscured by belief in women's "natural" reluctance to claim that they are any- thing other than "ordinary" and by the relentless myth of women's primary capacity as relational and supportive beings.

The lack of critical attention to women's autobiographies written

prior to World War II indicates, as feminist critics have recently
noted, the cultural privileging of male experience and the repression
of individual and collective female history. Nevertheless, in the
twentieth-century, and particularly in the decades since World War
II, more autobiographies by American women have been produced
than in any previous period of American letters, and an unprecedented number of critical works have emerged exploring the issues
of female autobiography. The increase suggests that American
women have moved steadily into positions of authority in both literary and academic life. According to Stone, "Autobiography now
forms an essential part of the network of feminine communication
and cultural critique which blossomed in the 1960s and the 1970s."[4]
And Lynn Z. Bloom asserts that female autobiographies such as
Mary McCarthy's *Memories of a Catholic Girlhood* succeeded in
doing what fictional feminist life narratives could not do: they redefine positive images of female selfhood and thus create new possibilities for women's lives.[5]

How and where have women discovered a territory in which to
construct a tradition of female autobiography? Working from the so-
called "margins" of American experience, what quests have American women writers enacted? What experiences could they record as
worthy of public consideration, since so few of them fought in wars,
led expeditions into uncharted regions, served as heads of govern-
ment, or built business empires? And what voice could women writers claim, if not a voice defined by dialectical tension between the
emergent sense of self constructed from within and the culture's definition of female identity as essentially subordinate to men?

Indeed, it would appear that the rugged individualist, militarist,
capitalist tradition associated with American male autobiography
relegates status to women on the basis of how their exploits "measure
up" to male standards. These standards impose silence upon those
women whose accomplishments reflect a lifetime commitment to
home, family, children, an internal rather than external career.
Thus, according to Patricia Meyer Spacks, as cultural narratives,
collectively and individually, women's autobiographies constitute "a
political statement: not only a personal but a political demand for
attention."[6] Autobiography, for women, becomes a form of social
protest, generating "psychic mobility and escape" from social oppression. Similarly, as Stone suggests, "because their status has so

often been defined as inferior and their freedom circumscribed by custom or law, women frequently are driven to treat personal history explicitly as an ideological instrument of liberation."[7]

Mary McCarthy's *Memories of a Catholic Girlhood* is not explicitly concerned with issues of gender. McCarthy does not take up feminism or women's rights as her banner, nor does she describe a struggle to overcome the limitations of femininity. Conventional family relationships through which women are generally defined and through which they are likely to derive a sense of identity play no part in the narrative development: the author's life is not explored in terms of relationship but in terms of self-awareness and self-actualization. Her roles as wife and mother are beyond the scope of the narrative, and are given little attention. Her roles as daughter to her parents and sister to her brothers are overshadowed by the early deaths of Roy and Tess McCarthy and by Mary's separation from her brothers when the children are distributed. In short, McCarthy is freed from the spaces women traditionally occupy in family-centered narrative. Virtually all of the relationships McCarthy discusses are unique for the keenly focused, yet emotionally detached critical scrutiny which they generate. Her memoirs are clearly and unconditionally intellectual, coming from an intellect totally absorbed in its own workings and motives, conspicuously longing to free the totality of self from the binding, blinding forces of family, love, and gender expectations.

But even if a woman writer plays down—or flat out denies—that her autobiographical act constitutes an act of social or political rebellion, a woman who tells her own story and claims her own piece of American history tenuously destabilizes the masculine name and the masculine institutions which are renamed from her perspective. Theorists Monique Wittig and Sande Zweig achieve this kind of crucial renaming of both the self and the world through a radical feminization of language. Among their inventions is a new definition of the word *word*: "to write one's life with one's blood."[8]

The direction the quest takes in Mary McCarthy's *Memories of a Catholic Girlhood* is back into the past, in search of the blood with which to write her life. McCarthy's quest is complicated by the fact that she has lost both her parents and the documentation of her past as well. The disinherited child thus aligns herself with a disinherited culture; her search represents the search of all women to discover a vital, meaningful connection to historical and social legacy. For the matriarchal heritage that has been erased, she invents a new history and establishes a pattern for the female quest, lighting out into the "previously forbidden territory in her own past."[9]

First published as separate pieces beginning in 1944, *Memories of a Catholic Girlhood* is a pioneering work in the formation of female quest narrative. McCarthy states at the outset, "Many a time, in the course of writing these memoirs, I have wished that I were writing fiction. The temptation to invent has been very strong."[10] Rather than fight this temptation, however, McCarthy's autobiographical fragments celebrate the power to invent, yet at the same time interrogate both the mechanisms of invention and the possibility of truthful representation. The autobiography renegotiates distinctions between truth and fiction by transforming the private search for the true self into a public confession of the gaps and absences, the out-and-out lies and marginal truths that always work in collusion with creativity and challenge our faith in a unified past or a unified subject.

In this regard, McCarthy's fictional autobiography betrays a familiar allegiance to modernist techniques and texts such as Proust's *Remembrance of Things Past*. However, from these gaps of evidence, these revealed margins of doubt, McCarthy's memoir also derives power and identity as a milestone text in the feminization of quest narrative. McCarthy conceives of the quest as a romantic journey to discover, and ultimately invent, the lost origins of female identity. The quest leads McCarthy into a territory once defined by faith in a "fixed" reality, a reality that is gradually reorganized and reclaimed by the interpretive processes of memory. "As the needs of the present prompt narrative interpretation of the past, [a] narrator's memory can yield a different 'reality,'" writes Joanne S. Frye, "a different chronology: a subversion of fixity, a reopening of cultural 'truth.'"[11] *Memories of a Catholic Girlhood* represents a woman's quest for self-definition that opposes categorical representations of linear, coherent, truthful selfhood, offering in its place "the possibility of at least retrospective control over experience—that control which women in their lives so often lack."[12]

McCarthy celebrates the formation of the subject as a process of slowly pulling together the scattered fragments and pieces that are themselves the very substance of identity: "What . . . family history I know has been pieced together from hearsay, from newspaper clippings, old photographs, and a sort of scrapbook journal . . ." (p. 6). By residing in the gaps between truth and fiction, past and present, McCarthy plays in the margins of uncertainty, timelessness, and un-reality—fringe forces which underlie both the modernist potential to reinvent historical accuracy and the feminist potential to refocus history on the representative fragmentation of the female subject. The "lighting out" adventure described in the text seeks not to resolve woman's historical absence but to acknowledge that the "true" history of the subject is always inscribed within its force.

The narrative sketches of the text are arranged out of chronological order, self-consciously stitched together by the subsequent addition of interchapters which offer the author's own gloss, an amalgam of critical commentary, confessions to having forgotten or altered the truth, reflections on the younger self writing of an even younger aspiring writer. The self-narrative process is under constant scrutiny; the mechanism of autobiography is exposed, revealing the process of self-creation involved. This process brings together two distinct phases of McCarthy's life: there is the adolescent McCarthy of the 1920s and the McCarthy of the 1940s and 1950s who assembled the pieces and wrote the interchapters for the text. This shifting time frame enacts a merger of these chapters of McCarthy's life, suggesting that the quest is a lifelong process, not a single, heroic episode or conclusive occasion.

McCarthy describes her attempt to reconstruct the fragments of the past as "a kind of quest," in which her brother, Kevin, and other relatives and friends have all taken part, "poring over albums with us, offering conjectures" (p. 6). Here the social element of the feminized quest is emphasized; in contrast to the traditional male pattern, in which the hero's quest is a solitary achievement benefiting a community at large, women's quests shape—and are equally shaped by—community involvement. Thus, the relational capacity that figures so prominently in patterns of female development is understood as a strength rather than an obstacle in the dialectical achievement of spiritual and social goals.

In reference to the writers who have influenced her, McCarthy admits, "I simply can't find my ancestors."[13] These words typically betray a fixation with the lost past, missing origins, absent precedents. McCarthy's quest begins as a search for these missing names and facts that might help her present a unified portrait of the past along with an equally coherent identity. However, her quest ultimately involves—and is fundamentally about—an acceptance of fragmentary knowledge as the proper condition of narrative self-portraiture. Just as important, the narrative journey allows the author to understand that the "truth," like the self, is always self-made, always a reinterpretation of images and events, a process of reorganizing the past and of altering both public and private perceptions.

"My father was a romancer," McCarthy writes, "and most of my memories of him are colored, I fear, by an untruthfulness that I must have caught from him, like one of the colds that ran around the family" (p. 11). As McCarthy begins to rename her experiences and describe the death of her parents, Roy and Tess McCarthy, during an outbreak of influenza, not only does the past become open to reinterpretation, but a cognitive gap is equated with a physical, corporeal loss of the parents. The autobiographical narrative becomes a quest to reclaim this lost ground, this lost knowledge. The quest involves a search for the bloodline, the raw material with which to validate one's life. Significantly, McCarthy recalls that at the age of six, in the aftermath of her parents' death (they died only days apart at McCarthy's paternal grandparents' house in Minneapolis), no one bothered to tell her what had happened to them, so that it took some time for her to absorb, through the atmosphere of mourning, the knowledge that her parents were gone for good. This primary experience of loss becomes immediately connected to silence, the unnameable loss, and becomes the experience which McCarthy must now name through the narrative process in order to assert linguistic control over her past and present self.

McCarthy was abandoned to the grim, disciplinary custody of her Aunt Margaret and Uncle Myers, and her account of her girlhood years vaguely recalls the plights of female orphans in nineteenth-century Victorian and sentimental novels. Enduring deprivation and physical abuse, McCarthy portrays herself as a dejected but stoic waif cut off from the affection and sense of specialness that she had been given by her mother and father. McCarthy's quest is to reconstitute the self by inscribing the clean slate of her familial identity. This erasure of the past—this void that parallels the lack of female literary tradition—becomes the major antagonist of the feminized quest to create heroic presence from historical absence. As Eileen Simpson observes in her personal and literary study of orphans, "Orphans lose the historian of their early years, and frequently the documentation as well."[14] This emptiness, this nameless condition, is corroborated by McCarthy's own words: "One great handicap to the task of recalling has been the fact of being an orphan. The chain of recollection—the collective memory of a family—has been broken. It is our parents, normally, who not only teach us our family history but who set us straight on our own childhood recollections, telling us that *this* cannot have happened the way we think it did . . ." (p. 5).

Rosalie Hewitt borrows Alfred Kazin's phrase, "to make a home for oneself on paper," in describing the central task of McCarthy's autobiographical expedition.[15] McCarthy succeeds in incorporating loss into this act of creation. For, as it stands to reason, orphanhood may be perceived as both a handicap and a blessing for the female hero when her quest involves a radical departure from conventions of the past and the burdens of tradition which assign women passive roles in the perpetuation of family name and legacy. The orphaned female represents, in this regard, perhaps the most utterly bereft and helpless object of fascination for the female imagination; deprived of all others to depend on, she must become more independent than gender codes normally require of her. In other words, she must become either a hero or a victim. Thus, for the female psyche engaged in the quest, the fact of being an orphan may be regarded as a somewhat dubious advantage. For McCarthy, heroism is less a revolutionary gesture than a matter of survival as she searches both with longing, and with caution, for those influences which contributed to her development. "Was it a good thing . . ." she wonders, "that our parents were 'taken away,' as if by some higher design?" (p. 17). Indeed, the orphanage of the soul may be the ideal vantage point from which to create a new history and a new identity. Myth, modern psychology, literary theory, anthropological and cultural theories have all betrayed a primal fascination with orphanhood: a desire to kill or to find oneself suddenly free of the past—a past which threatens to fix and determine identity beyond the individual determination to recreate oneself. To be an orphan is to receive as one's legacy the solitary purpose of self-invention. And if one of the central tasks of feminist criticism is to mark and interpret the strategies with which women writers have forged authentic female identities, pursued culturally unacceptable longings and aspirations, and rebelled against male-perpetuated gender codes, then the factual or fictional declaration of oneself as an orphan seems predicated upon the necessary and desirable conditions for feminist achievement. The admission of orphanhood may thus constitute, for women, a choice of identity, a declaration of freedom that both defines and defies the dispossession that society imposes on her because of gender. Orphanhood is, at very least, the stuff of powerful fantasy for women longing to experience complete independence and autonomy in the world.

In McCarthy's narrative, selective and collective memory merge; mutual interpretation opens a path to personal salvation as McCarthy elicits the help of her brothers and their wives and others in the quest to discover the key to her past. The death of Roy and Tess McCarthy blocks entrance to a territory, the exploration of which ultimately requires a bold maneuver across the frontier that distinguishes fact from fiction. The text is a searching mind's engagement in openly validating the saving function of selective memory. McCarthy defines her development as a process of gathering the scattered details of her past, and with these accumulated bits slowly, artfully piecing together a representation of self. The choices she necessarily makes define a relationship to an uncertain, indifferent past, a history composed essentially of doubts rather than certainties. Did Uncle Myers hide the tin butterfly at McCarthy's table setting, or was this idea suggested to her by a professor at Vassar? Was Roy McCarthy a periodic drunkard, and was his extravagant spending of family funds the reason why his parents brought him back to Minneapolis in the midst of a major flu epidemic? *Memories of a Catholic Girlhood* presents an effort to authenticate the choices one makes in negotiating the mysteries of a territory one would invent to call home. In the margins where McCarthy stakes her claim, she inscribes not only a map of the unknowable past but an interpretation of the map which marks the choices she has made in the breaking of this new ground.

"Looking back, I see that it was religion that saved me" (p. 18), McCarthy admits. From the Roman Catholic Church she gets what family could not provide her—a sense of belonging, of participating in a ritual drama. "To care for the quarrels of the past, to identify oneself passionately with a cause that became, politically speaking, a losing cause with the birth of the modern world, is to experience a kind of straining against reality, a rebellious nonconformity . . ." (p. 25). Identifying with the Church and its history, McCarthy claims a part in a romance with the past that supplants lost and shattered familial ritual. She is thus able to derive through her association with the Church some faith in an illusive vision of unity and continuity, a fundamental trust in the eternal presence of the Mother and the Father. In this sense, the Church becomes for McCarthy a substitute for the parents who are lost. McCarthy's eventual loss of faith, her rebellion against the institution of the Sacred Hearts Convent, represents the essential ritual of separation and individuation from the parents, the fulfillment of the Oedipal drama. The quest toward self-discovery involves, finally, a motion away from the authority and protection of the Catholic Church; in challenging its doctrine, McCarthy begins the process of differentiation and self-naming. By directing her rebellion against the microcosmic society of the Sacred Hearts Convent—a society of women who have sacrificed themselves in the name of the Father—McCarthy assumes a subversive position against such privileged complicity with patriarchal myth and law.

McCarthy writes, "If you are born and brought up a Catholic, you have absorbed a good deal of world history and the history of ideas before you are twelve, and it is like learning a language early, the effect is indelible" (p. 24). To have one's history is to inherit one's language, but to lose one's history is to have to invent for oneself a new language. "The important thing," she continues, "is to know the past of a foreign country in such detail that it becomes one's own" (p. 25). McCarthy's desire to both belong to and possess her history parallels the textual impulse behind naming oneself and creating the text of one's life. In this regard, McCarthy's text speaks for women writers engaged in the process of discovering their own history, a history neither expressed nor expressible in the language or sanctioned texts of male-dominant culture.

Memories of a Catholic Girlhood is a symbolic voyage into a foreign country—her own life—the history of which, McCarthy learns, she must invent in order to resist the imposture of conventional belief. As Frye has argued convincingly, "Saying 'I am' is itself one of the most powerful expressions of a woman's capacity to resist cul-

tural definitions: the narrating 'I' both defines herself and subverts
entrapment in difference."[16] When she loses her Catholic faith, Mc-
Carthy rejects the symbolic Father, individuates from the symbolic
Mother, and is freed to discover and rename herself. What McCarthy
discovers is that, through the quest to reinterpret the past, one invents oneself and simultaneously invests oneself in the currency of
new faith in the powers of self-creation. Thus, McCarthy's quest remains throughout an act of devotion; "true" devotion, likewise, requires an exploration beyond the fixed discourse of orthodoxy.

Looking back over women's autobiographies of the past several
decades, Estelle Jelinek acknowledges that while contemporary
women write "with the assurance and command usually associated
with men's autobiographies, we still find in most women's autobiographies a sense . . . of being mavericks, outcasts, or, at the
least, rebels against what society expects of them."[17] In *Memories of
a Catholic Girlhood* rebellion against the characteristics that define
female heroism—virtue and moral righteousness—is expressed in
the fundamental conflict of McCarthy's life—a conflict represented
by her attraction to both Caesar and Catiline, a commitment to rebellion and to law. "I have battled, usually without avail, against a
temptation to do something which only I knew was bad, being swept
on by a need to preserve outward appearances and to live up to
other people's expectations of me" (pp. 20–21). This battle, which
McCarthy sees as central to her life, can be read as an analogue for
the concurrent conflicts that form the narrative—conflicts between
personal and public duty, confession and deception, self and other.
"These two opposed duties were rushing inflexibly toward each
other, like two trains on the same track" (p. 161). The threatening
collision of impulses suggests the dilemma women writers have
faced as their efforts to adapt and redefine the patterns of the quest
invariably create tensions between the desire to subvert the systems
that withhold power from women and the desire to comply with the
patriarchal demand that women, in order to be "heroic," appear selfless, giving, and eager to please. The public and personal demands
of female heroism are thus shown to be in direct opposition, as
McCarthy's description of her first holy communion serves to illus-
trate. In her excitement on the morning of her first communion,
McCarthy forgets to fast and drinks a sip of water. Horrified by her
sin, she must decide whether to confess her impurity and refuse

communion or to pretend for the sake of all who have been anticipating the event that nothing has happened. The ensuing moral crisis requires a choice between confessing the personal spirit and sustaining the public spirit. Like Huck Finn, whose own definition of heroism demands finally that he break society's rules, McCarthy decides, "All right, then, I'll go to hell," and accepts communion "in a state of outward holiness and inward terror" (p. 20). Her decision openly acknowledges the paradox of moral "goodness" and the social function of heroism. For the woman author, this paradox becomes an issue not only as she departs from conventional notions of female goodness, but as she assumes the authority to control and manipulate her public image. To lie "not for selfish reasons but in the interests of the community, like a grown-up responsible person," unites an act of self-invention that guides the personal quest with an act of public heroism which suggests dissension in the face of the law (p. 162).

Like Jean Stafford remembering her portrayal of Good Deeds in *Everyman*, McCarthy experiences in the process of her education a lack of viable roles and role models for imagining female rebelliousness: "Many women seek new visions of power and personhood and do not wish to become like men in their struggle for equality and justice."[18] McCarthy can discover no female precedents for her quest, and yet she feels she has "a duty to break the rules and take all offered risks" (p. 161). Seeking to identify with Catiline, McCarthy writes, "To my mind, [he] was not only a hero—he was me" (p. 145). In "The Blackguard," the young McCarthy is honored when during a lesson on the Romantic poets, Madame Barclay offers a comparison to the class, suggesting that Mary is "just like Lord Byron, brilliant but unsound" (p. 94). Although McCarthy reads the representation as "a declaration of love," her grandfather, hearing of the incident, is enraged at the damaging association "of his innocent granddaughter with that degenerate blackguard, Byron": "For my grandfather, history had interposed no distance between Lord Byron and himself. Though the incestuous poet had died forty years before my grandfather was born, the romantic perspective was lacking" (pp. 94–95). Insisting that Madame Barclay publicly renounce the association, Grandfather Preston unwittingly reopens the search that his granddaughter had hoped to resolve by cultivating an image for herself founded on an identification with the rebel poet.

In "C'est le Premier Pas Qui Coute," McCarthy recounts her en-rollment at the Sacred Hearts Convent School and her painful recog-nition of a spiritual void as she realizes that in the society of the convent, unlike her previous school, she is an outsider, a "nobody." Desperate to win the attention and admiration of her peers, she schemes to publicly lose her faith, just long enough to gain the cen-ter of attention, and then dramatically rediscover it in time to receive communion at an upcoming retreat.

After declaring her loss to Madam Macillvra, "*Ma Mere*, I have lost my faith," McCarthy is sent somberly to her room where she is told to wait to speak to Father Dennis. "I had not realized that what I had said was so serious . . . for the first time it occurred to me that I would have to have arguments to make my doubts sound real" (p. 113). And it is while in her room, preparing these arguments, that she realizes, having for the first time carefully examined the issue of faith from all sides, that she *has truly* lost her belief in the divinity of Christ. "I was trying with all my power, to feel faith, if only as a public duty, but the more I tapped and tested myself, the more I was forced to recognize that there was no belief inside me. My very soul had fled . . ." (p. 122). Invention for the sake of personal gain thus redefines the true self and becomes a public drama that threatens to expose the vulnerable structure of unyielding trust in the social order. The lie is transformed into truth. The invented life becomes the life on record, the life as it was truly experienced. The message conveyed in these dislocations of value is that fabrication constitutes the road to truth; the way of self-invention leads to au-thentic faith, not in only in the self but in the world it occupies and recreates.

As McCarthy expounds on the implicit contradictions of church doctrine, the intellectual quality of her arguments fills her with self-pride; she waits eagerly for her interview with Father Dennis, hoping to engage with him in a theological debate of great merit. This trans-ference of love from object to subject marks McCarthy's true spiri-tual awakening, as do the ensuing conversations with Father Dennis, from whom the young scholar McCarthy is able to get only evasive replies and patronizing admonitions. "These priests," she writes, "seemed to imagine that you could do nothing for yourself, that everything was from inheritance and from reading . . ." (p. 122). Substitute "a woman" for the second-person pronoun and the implicit gender conflict of McCarthy's statement becomes clear. The powers of naming and interpreting the *logos* are believed to be male processes, or faculties, which preserve knowledge and law to be passed on from men to men. To whom, then, can a young woman turn in order to discover her own inheritance, her own power, and her own literature of experience? "What, I asked myself shrewdly, was the church trying to hide from me?" (p. 117). As McCarthy challenges theological doctrine, she reveals the inconsistencies and spaces of uncertainty, and thus begins to dethrone patriarchal logic by dismantling its discourse. Or, in Lacanian terms, she blasphemes the symbolic phallus, empowered by its concealment behind the mask of absolute knowledge.

In her second interview with Father Heeney, McCarthy is at last able to exact *his* confession that there is, in fact, a blind spot between reason and belief, "a little gap that we have to fill with faith" (p. 123). "So there *was* a gap, then," McCarthy exclaims. This revelation, this gap, informs the process of the remaining narrative. This gap parallels the "break in the collective chain" that impels the quest. It corresponds to the line between truth and fiction that the autobiography negotiates, as well as the margin between realism and romance that guides memory toward a reinterpretation of the past, openly confessing to contradiction, irresolution, absence of certainty. At the conclusion of these debates, McCarthy decides to pretend for the benefit of others that she has regained her faith. Her decision reminds us once again that one cannot abstract a spiritual quest from a social context. The explorations of the private soul occur always in direct relationship to social and community concerns. This remains a recurring issue throughout *Memories of a Catholic Girlhood*; McCarthy's confessions insist that her lies were always told in the interest of what she discerned as the "public" good. In this sense, fabrication, like the quest toward self-invention, is presented as a noble, heroic gesture.

Confession, like the autobiographical act, is an act of naming and therefore an assertion of the power to transform the self and the world within a symbolic order. Women's quests toward a naming of the self as subject must begin with a confession of the nameless past, the consequence of externally imposed silence, an awakening to the contradictions alive in the powers they privilege when they accept names that mark them as the property of men. Inherent in the re-

ification of female difference which the symbolic order prescribes is
the assumption that a self-actualized female identity is in itself a
misnomer. Supporting the fundamental binary logic inherent in this
order, Michael Ragussis defines human beings as "divided between
those who rule by naming and those who rule by being named." [19]
Dispossessed from "proper nomenclature," a woman's name therefore "dramatizes the fundamental non-presence of the female subject, even as it asserts itself discursively and strives towards an always impossible self-possession." [20]

When a woman refuses her name she defies definition and lights
out to a territory known only to her now as absence. Equipped with
the wrong alphabet, all the words incongruous with the logic of this
landscape, the stories never told about it, she abandons herself only
to find herself in need of something more than the "dream of a common language," which Adrienne Rich described, but an alert and
vivid representation of this soul in flight, a name specific to this
experience.

When a woman renames herself, she not only renames the world
but calls herself into battle—at last armed with an authentic "primacy" of the female self—with the existing symbolic order. In *Diving Deep and Surfacing: Women Writers on Spiritual Quest*, Carol
Christ proposes that the act of renaming constitutes the final phase of
women's quests toward a self-realized identity. Unlike the patterns
of the male monomyth which Joseph Campbell defined in *Hero with
a Thousand Faces*, women's spiritual and social quests are predicated on nonlinear, cyclical journeys. According to Christ's schema,
the female quest involves first an experience of nothingness and self-
negation, followed by an awakening, a grounding in the powers of
being through connection to natural or mythical forces. Finally, the
female quester's new perception of self and her relationship to the
world culminates in an act of new naming. As women claim this autonomous control over their destinies, they redefine their cosmic as
well as their social power. As Christ observes, "Participating in a
ritual of the new naming brings women's experiences and visions out
into the open and . . . transforms them from private to public reality." Finally, what is stressed through the rituals of naming is "the
dynamic quality of power." [21]

Sections of Mary McCarthy's *Memories of a Catholic Girlhood* may
be read sequentially as a patterning after the model of the quest that

Carol Christ describes. The series of incidents McCarthy recreates reflects her experience of nothingness in the early death of her parents, her spiritual and social awakening in her loss of Christian faith, and her recognition of the power dynamic implied not only in the name but in the process of renaming.

"Names" explores McCarthy's struggle toward claiming a language of her own, a mode of representation outside the dominant symbolic order which would confer upon her the status of the named rather than the power of the namer. "Names have more significance for Catholics than they do for other people," she writes. "The saint a child is named for is supposed to serve, literally, as a model . . . your name is your fortune and it tells you what you are or must be" (p. 129). As part of the subversive process of female self-naming which the autobiographical act represents, McCarthy recalls two related incidents from her Catholic boarding-school days. Each of these incidents involves a misnaming, and each contributes consequently to the adolescent McCarthy's increasingly frustrated efforts to inscribe her authentic presence within the social sphere of the convent.

The first incident concerns McCarthy's determined campaign to make friends with the two self-appointed wits of the ninth grade. This pair delight in exercising their power over the eighth-grade class by devising cryptic nicknames for those students in whom they see some quality worth immortalizing. Finding herself the victim of one of these inventions, McCarthy is given the nickname C.Y.E. The name quickly spreads through the school, and soon everyone except McCarthy knows what the letters C.Y.E. stand for. The value of the name remains obvious to all but her, even in spite of her imaginative efforts to interpret the mysterious significance. "In the convent I was certain that it stood for something horrible . . . some aspect of myself that the world could see and I couldn't, like a sign pinned on my back" (p. 135). The nickname becomes, for McCarthy, an annihilating force which works to split the subject into an opposed public and private image. Thus divided against herself, McCarthy writes, "This name . . . solidified my sense of wrongness, it turned me into an outsider . . . And it made everyone laugh" (p. 135).

This frustrating situation is rendered with a humorous and slightly self-mocking edge. Nevertheless, the sense of fraudulence and entrapment McCarthy experiences along with the nickname foreshadows her emergent rebellion against an all-encompassing symbolic order, the purpose of which is to frame her. The nickname corroborates McCarthy's growing suspicion that she simply is not able to "fit into the convent pattern." Consequently, the self-image McCarthy must struggle against is an image based on misreadings and symbolic patterns that are incongruous with her own evolving terminology of the self and her own patterns of development.

While the nickname continues to haunt her, another incident requires an even greater sacrifice of linguistic control over experience. Awakening one morning to find her sheets specked with blood, McCarthy notices a small cut on her leg which had reopened during the night. Knowing how picky the sisters are about cleanliness, she takes the stained bedsheet to one of the sisters so that she can get a clean substitute. However, the sister misreads the blood signs and, assuming that a lecture on the menstrual cycle is now in order, immediately ushers McCarthy along to speak with the Mother Superior. Mother Superior, next in line to read the evidence, accepts no explanations, in spite of McCarthy's pleading and insistence that she has simply reopened a cut with her toenail. Convinced beyond any margin of doubt that McCarthy has started her period, Mother Superior solemnly provides her with a sanitary belt and napkin. "There's nothing to be afraid of," she intones ceremoniously. "You have become a woman."

Thus named again, not only against her will this time but against her biological capacity, McCarthy accepts silence as the only solution to her entrapment. "I was in the grip of a higher authority," she writes, "which almost had the power to persuade me that it was right and I was wrong . . . [t]here was no use fighting the convent. I had to pretend to have become a woman" (pp. 133–134).

Assuming the name of woman under false pretenses, McCarthy proceeds to reopen the cut on her leg every twenty-eight days and bleed on her napkin in compliance with the sisters' wish that she sign herself with the name they have given her. What the sisters perceive to be a biological initiation becomes, however, McCarthy's awakening to the limitations of female identity. She finds herself, thus, in the very awkward position of having to sign, in her own blood, an autograph which is not genuine. The sign represents, like the nickname C.Y.E., her dispossession from the order of the convent as well the conventional ordering of experience. "The simplest thing I did," she writes, "like asking for a clean sheet, entrapped me in consequences that I never could have predicted" (p. 136). Expressing awareness of her imprisonment in someone else's text, McCarthy places "Names" in the tradition of female plots and narratives that suggest, according to Gilbert and Gubar, woman's primary identification with the "madwoman in the attic." Indeed, this condition may be defined as the fate of all women dispossessed by patriarchy. To become imprisoned in a false identity is to have her life-essence, her body's own blood, promptly interpreted for her. Powerless to convince anyone of the actual meaning of the text, McCarthy becomes imprisoned in her white sheets like the woman trapped in the yellow wallpaper of Charlotte Perkins Gilman's definitive nightmare.

The representations of acute conflict over names reflects a developing awareness of female identity as incongruous with the conventional patterns and images of female representation. Renaming *themselves* becomes the symbolic act by which women free themselves from entrapment in narrative forms and social codes. The social and literary conventions that enforce the lawful naming of women thus support the customary suppression of the female, literally in a word. These institutions succeed not simply by the act of naming, but through the internalization of the name, for when women accept the false identities built around them, they become their own jailers. Symbolically then, as well as literally, the most radical gesture of self-possession that a woman can make is to shake off her name and choose her own, thus acknowledging her freedom from both an external social order and an internal psychic structure that no longer accepts an inappropriate self-image. As Frye has observed, "Patriarchal oppression bears heavily on individual women's possibilities for self-identification," for their primary source of identification remains always with the father and consequently becomes rooted in difference. [22]

In "Names" there is no dramatic fulfillment of the self-naming ritual. The adolescent McCarthy accepts these misnomers until she can escape "the names that did not seem to me any more mine but to have been imposed on me by others" (p. 137). However, the function of the chapter is to enact one small step in the gradual motion toward renaming that the text as a whole represents. In this particular fragment, the multiplicity of names given, assumed, assigned, and rejected throughout the chapter suggests, as Ragussis explains, that "an individual's history requires a set of names, or a series of renamings that signal the different stages of a life story or fictional plot. The 'true name,' then, often functions as a series of names, a composite name . . . one must take them all . . . to have one's history."[23] In "Names," Mary McCarthy defined the processes that recent feminist theorists have identified as fundamental in the female's quest for self-definition. To write one's life in blood, to name oneself after a memory of loss, is to begin the search for a new name, to declare, finally, with lasting effect, "I am. I name myself." McCarthy indicates this emerging strength in the conclusion to "Names," where she chooses a meaning of her name that expresses her authentic response to the lack of power she has experienced: "I preferred to think that Mary meant 'bitter' rather than 'star of the sea'" (p. 137).

"The one duty we owe to history is to rewrite it," said Oscar Wilde.[24] In *Memories of a Catholic Girlhood*, Mary McCarthy suggests that our only duty to the self is to reinvent it. Her autobiography is an act of the imagination that strives to recover the lost material of her original birth so that she can reproduce a version of the self and, through this process, be "reborn." Like the spectacular train derailment in Marilynne Robinson's *Housekeeping*, the death of McCarthy's parents sends her own journey off the routine track. Both disasters consequently break the "collective chain" of memory and call for a new kind of hero—a hero dispossessed from legend—to retrace a lost path back into the dark continent of the female psyche.

The mystery of Fingerbone lake in *Housekeeping* finds its equivalent in McCarthy's Grandmother Preston, both forbidden bodies representing the dark depth of the unseen past. In "Ask Me No Questions," the final section of the narrative, McCarthy betrays a fascination with her grandmother's bodily domain and her daily private ritual of anointment followed always by the public ritual of display during her routine shopping trips. In the course of the chapter, McCarthy refers to this corporeal presence as "the cult of a relic," a "wealth of fleshly, material detail," "and the cult object around which our household revolved" (pp. 241, 266, 225). Although some critics see McCarthy's grandmother functioning as a surrogate for Mary in the concluding section, she appears within the context of the feminized quest as the sacred container which holds the key to the past, the seed of new life. This image is supported rhetorically by McCarthy's selection of words connoting birth. Recalling her grandmother's passion for apricots, she recalls, "Now I, too, am fond of them, and whenever I choose one from a plate, I think of my grandmother's body, full-fleshed, bland, smooth, and plump, cushioning in itself, close held—a secret, like the flat brown seed of the apricot" (p. 225).

Thus, the autobiography conceptualizes history as the body of the mother, a body one must reenter in order to be reborn. This quest to reenter the mother's body may be understood as a strategy in the feminization of the quest, but also in the grass-roots feminization of women's history, a process revolutionizing male-dominant history's claim to speak of universal experience, a process qualifying its worth as applicable to only a fraction of those whose lives are inscribed within its scope. Thus, in *Memories of a Catholic Girlhood*, the object of women's collective struggles and the object of one woman's quest merge: to reclaim and renovate the landscape of memory, to create identity through rebirth and renaming, to set a precedent for women's power to make and choose the self. McCarthy clearly articulated this goal during an interview conducted in 1961. When asked about her novelistic theme of the "fragmented unplaceability of the human personality," she replied: "But I was very young then. I think I'm not really interested in the quest for the self anymore. Oh, I suppose everyone continues to be interested in the quest for the self, but what you feel when you're older, I think, is that—how to express this—that you really must *make* the self. It's absolutely useless to look for it, you won't find it, but . . . you finally begin in some sense to make and to choose the self you want."[25]

5. "The Spark from the Outside World"

Anne Moody's *Coming of Age in Mississippi*

When we are children, growing up in our parents' care, we await the spark from the outside world. Sometimes our parents provide it—if we are lucky—sometimes it comes from another source far from home. We sit, paralyzed, surrounded by our anxiety and dread, hoping we will not have to grow up into the narrow world and ways we see about us. We are hungry for a life that turns us on; we yearn for a knowledge of living that will save us from innocuous lives that resemble death. We look for signs in every strange event; we search for heroes in every unknown face.
—WALKER, *IN SEARCH OF OUR MOTHER'S GARDENS*

In "Teaching *Black-Eyed Susans:* An Approach to the Study of Black Women Writers," Mary Helen Washington suggests several different methods for teaching contemporary black American women's writing. One of these methods, a "personal historical" view, is recommended by Alice Walker. Her approach traces the evolution of black women's writings through three distinct yet interconnected historical and psychological stages: suspension, assimilation, and emergence.[1] These chronological stages follow the development of black women in a "series of movements," leading from portrayals of black women who are totally immobilized by racial and sexual oppression, to portrayals of self-aware women who are nevertheless stunted by psychic alienation and a lack of space in society, to portrayals of women finally able to claim power over conditions and improve their lives. Washington describes the women of this third category, the "Emergent Women": "They are women coming just to the edge of a new awareness and making the first tentative steps into an uncharted region. And, although they are more fully conscious of their political and psychological oppression and more capable of creating new options for themselves, they must undergo a harsh initiation before they are ready to occupy and claim any new territory."[2]

Although Walker does not speak specifically in terms of women's quests, her proposal does suggest a structural pattern for the feminized quest-romance. Her outline is important not only because it illuminates a history of images of black women but because it addresses and locates a convergence of a race-specific and gender-specific "lighting out" theme in black women's literature.

In the twentieth century, the stories of black women's struggles recorded by such American writers as Walker herself, Zora Neale Hurston, Gwendolyn Brooks, Audre Lorde, Louise Meriwether, Ann Petry, Paule Marshall, Toni Morrison, Ntozake Shange, and others substantiate a powerful collective affirmation of black women's journeys toward self-realization in a society that offers limited options for their futures, undervalues their potential, ignores their contributions, distorts their history, and obstructs their rights as free-thinking individuals.

How do black women voyage out into such a world? Indeed, to be black and female is to be twice dispossessed in American culture. Gender and race are double obstacles in the black woman's quest toward a self-determined identity. While portraits of female quests often present bleak prospects for optimistic white heroines, black female questers often endure even grimmer journeys toward inevitable recognition of abandoned dreams and lost hope. Thus, as Toni Morrison's Pecola Breedlove finds refuge in madness, Louise Meriwether's Francie Coffin is left to utter "shit" as her final word, a requiem upon her future. In addition to race and gender, poverty works against these protagonists. With no means of saving themselves from their desperate circumstances and hopeless surroundings, their quests are halted before they're even begun. In *Daddy Was a Numbers Runner*, Francie's rite of passage is her acceptance of silence and immobility. "There was nothing else to say," she realizes. "Either you was a whore . . . or you worked in a laundry or did day's work . . . or had a baby every year."[3] Francie lacks both the psychic and social mobility that enabled a young Mary McCarthy to even think of attending Vassar; not only are Francie's efforts discouraged but her dreams as well. Consequently, understanding the evolution of feminized quests requires the realization that racial and

class politics represent equally powerful antagonists which the questing woman must overcome in order to emerge from her quest with
identity, courage, ambition, and self intact.

While black American women's literature should be read as part
of a wide tradition of American women's literature, it also maintains
its own integrity, constitutes its own tradition, and engages its own
specific battles, myths, metaphors, and symbols. "Black writers
seem always involved in a moral and/or physical struggle," writes
Alice Walker, "the result of which is expected to be some kind of
larger freedom. . . ."[4] A positive portrait of a successful quest to
this "larger freedom" means transcending not only the reality of social prejudice, economic disadvantage, and political oppression, but
for the imagination it means transcending the stereotypical images of
black women and black family life that have worked to reduce characters to embodiments of white myths and fears: the prototypical
black matriarch or "mammy"; the black sex goddess; the "evil"
black woman; the unwed welfare mother. When we speak of woman's
quest, we speak of a potential for growth and industry largely determined by the culturally available images which make it possible to
assert one's influence in the world and to imagine oneself a subject.
Historically and psychologically, these stereotypes have compromised the authenticity of the black female subject and her spiritual
and social quest. When a black woman speaks of the self, when she
breaks the silence that a legacy of invisibility has imposed upon her,
she undertakes a truly courageous, dangerous, and radical act.
Thus, to present a black woman's quest for selfhood is to reveal
power and promise where it has rarely been shown to exist before.

A key contribution to this revolutionary literary movement is
Anne Moody's autobiographical narrative *Coming of Age in Mississippi*. Moody's autobiography is a journey toward active participation
in the world. The social unrest that defines the civil rights era finds a
powerful parallel in the inner turmoil of Anne Moody's struggle toward maturity in the rural South. Her autobiography stands as a
major historical document of the civil rights movement as well as a
key contribution to the feminization of the quest; in *Coming of Age
in Mississippi* the personal crisis of female identity merges with the
political crisis of national identity: the movement becomes a metaphor for the feminized quest as well as the motion toward human
awakening to the destructive politics of race. Thus, Moody's nar-

rative establishes an active dialectic between internal and external development, or social and spiritual quest.

Moody's solitary voice articulates a determined quest for communal freedom among Mississippi blacks: the narrative remains very much a document of the self in its dynamic relationship to the world. The autobiography connects the strength, aggressiveness, and courage of a young, poor, black woman with a revolutionary moment in history. Moody's journey parallels the struggle of a people, and ultimately the struggle of a nation being impelled toward change. Her personal loss of innocence reflects the loss of national innocence, the dawning of the turbulent 1960s and a violent shift in ideological awareness. This bold politicization of the classic pattern of the heroic quest, in combination with the radical subversion that Moody's heroism suggests, makes *Coming of Age in Mississippi* a revolutionary and unprecedented achievement in the feminization of the quest.

Rather than a Colorado cattle ranch or a Sacred Hearts Convent on Puget Sound, Anne Moody's quest is set in rural Mississippi. She is the eldest child of poor tenant farmers who work the cotton fields of a Mr. Carter, whose stately white house overlooks the rotted wooden shacks of his black laborers.

Like the quest in *Memories of a Catholic Girlhood*, Moody's begins with an incident of familial injustice that sets the stage for the call to action of the hero. Paralleling Mary McCarthy's recollection in "The Tin Butterfly" of her cruel Uncle Myer, Moody's account of physical abuse at the hands of her young uncle, George Lee, provides evidence of the hero's education in powerlessness, victimization, and injustice. George Lee, in an effort to get out of baby-sitting for Anne and her infant sister, sets fire to the Moodys' shack, burning the walls and scant furnishings. When Moody's father demands to know how the fire got started, George Lee accuses Anne of playing with matches. Unable to convince her father of her innocence, Anne is whipped violently by her father, who, frustrated and desperate, releases his own rage on his helpless daughter. In this scene, the hero's destiny is foreshadowed: her quest will be to right the wrongs committed against the innocent, to seek justice in a world of injustice.

When Moody's father leaves his pregnant wife and children for another woman, Moody's mother is left with sole responsibility for supporting the family. Moody's "childhood" is cut short as she, too,

assumes the role of mother to her younger siblings. Her life becomes
a series of movements as her mother changes jobs, uprooting the
family from one run-down shack to another; constant dislocation and
alienation foreshadow Moody's radical departure for the heroic
quest. "It seemed we were always moving," she writes. "Everytime
it was a house on some white man's place and every time it was a
room and a kitchen."[5]

When her mother begins working as a domestic for white families,
Moody is given her first opportunities to compare her life and her
family with the lives and families of the white children whose needs
now seem to take precedence over hers. These recognitions occur
gradually; at first, she enjoys playing with the white children who
willingly share their many first-rate toys with her. But then she begins to wonder about the apparent inequity of their circumstances.
Slowly her eyes open to the difference between the spacious, well-
groomed neighborhoods of whites and the shoddy, unkempt neighborhoods where blacks live crammed together in shacks without in-
door plumbing. Her awakening to such very different circumstances
causes her to consider her own inferiority to white children. When
she attends a movie with white friends, Moody is suddenly separated
from them by an usher who scorns her arrogance and sends her up-
stairs to the Negro section. Here she experiences a painful jolt,
much like the shock Hurston's Janie undergoes as a child when a
photograph impresses upon her for the first time the fact that she is
black.

> . . . things were not the same. I had never really thought of
> them as white before. Now all of a sudden they were white and
> their whiteness made them better than me. I now realized that
> not only were they better than me because they were white, but
> everything they owned and everything connected with them was
> better than what was available to me. . . . "There is a secret
> to it besides being white," I thought. Then my mind got all
> wrapped up in trying to uncover that secret. (P. 39)

Thus, Moody begins her quest to discover and confront the mystery
of whiteness that suggests her condition of social namelessness and
that, according to Kimberly A. Benston, "both repels and attracts"
the hero in a Melvillian quest to discover the truth of the self.[6] This

mystery comes to stand for the seed at the center of life, the core of selfhood that Moody's quest must ultimately discover.

Moody reinvents the scheme of the quest as a pattern for reclaiming the history of black America. In keeping with Walker's identification of the "Emergent Woman," Moody claims a brave new territory and presents herself as a new kind of female hero, one who is not paralyzed by racial difference but empowered by it, impelled forward into the world. Moody's call to adventure translates into a call to recreate heroism through a female's participation in a movement to recreate society and myth. As readers witness the gradual opening of Moody's eyes, Moody herself realizes the gradual opening of a heroic destiny ahead of her.

The church, around which much of Southern black culture coheres, is a powerful source of identity for the black community in general and for the community of women in particular. Baptism symbolizes a spiritual rebirth—an essential rite of passage into this community, a spiritual bonding with the forces of salvation. For Moody, however, baptism only promises to bind her to a past that she yearns to escape. Moody's account of her begrudging baptism and the subsequent changing of her name from Essie Mae to Anne represents the two interconnected acts of unnaming and naming, death and spiritual/political rebirth.

Moody's preference to be baptized at the progressive, politically active Centreville church instead of at her mother's old-fashioned, country church suggests her symbolic disjunction from the beliefs and conventions of the past. Her baptism fulfills her mother's desire for continuity rather than her own wish for a bolder, more active black community. While Mount Pleasant encourages its congregation to be passive, to pray for rewards in the afterlife rather than fight to change their lives in the present, Centreville Baptist has a lively youth group, a boisterous congregation, and a preacher with the glamorous reputation of having been imprisoned once for killing a man. Waging a passive rebellion against her mother's insistence on the Mount Pleasant church, Moody oversleeps on the morning of the ceremony, "accidently" rips her baptism dress, and arrives at the church an hour late.

Throughout the ceremony, Moody becomes increasingly frustrated and sickened by the hypocrisy underlying the occasion. As her forced participation continues, so her anger rises. As she waits to be led into the river to be baptized, Moody sees large piles of cow manure floating on the water. "The thought of being ducked under that water made me want to vomit," she recalls. "As I waded into the water, I could feel the mud sticking to my legs. I was mad as hell, and I heard Sister Jones' voice singing, 'Nothing but the righteous . . .' along with the rest, I thought, 'Nothing but the *righteous*. Some Shit!'" (pp. 78–79).

With this exclamation, Moody brings the spiritual experience back down to earth where she feels the responsibility of the church should lie. In the rejection of her baptism, Moody breaks with both her spiritual father and her biological mother, figures representing both spirit and flesh. Moody thus denigrates and reforms her ties to a "fragmented familial past."[7] Her unveiling causes a parallel denunciation of what she perceives to be Mount Pleasant's role in the black community. Moody sees angrily where her mother's church has encouraged blacks to be complacent victims in a society that encourages their sense of powerlessness; she sees the admonitions against sin as unrealistic and repressive in a community of people whose desires and spirits have already been beaten out of them by racism and poverty. Thus, in spite of the filthy, murky waters, Moody's baptism grants her a moment of clear vision. Finally, she sees through the illusions of her mother's faith and into her own powers.

Gloria Hull has pointed out that "like any politically disenfranchised group, Black women could not exist consciously until we began to name ourselves."[8] Moody's act of unnaming and the adoption of the new name signals her rejection of forced participation in the dominant society's symbolic order. According to Benston, the "simultaneous unnaming and naming—affirming at once autonomy and identification in relation to the past" presents "a means of passing from one mode of representation to another, of breaking the rhetoric and 'plot' of influence, of distinguishing the self from all else."[9] Moody is baptized in the name of Essie Mae, a name which she feels is "suitable for a cow or a hog" (p. 110). She must, therefore, lose the slave name Essie Mae in order to displace the power of white society and free herself from forced bondage.

Moody's new name comes to her as the result of a clerical error on her birth certificate; the document indicates that her name is Annie Mae instead of Essie. When she discovers the mistake, Moody eagerly adopts the new name as her new identity. The change suggests at once white America's erroneous perception of black identity and Moody's new position in relation to the world. Although her mother refuses to address her by the new name, Annie Mae promptly informs her teachers and friends that from now on she is no longer to be called Essie Mae but Anne Moody.

This rejection of her old name coincides with another departure from the ways of the past. Although farming has been in her family's blood for generations, Moody rejects the working of the land. She respects her mother's covenant with the earth, her faith in the charity of the soil: "She would kick her foot into the soil and say, 'Boy, you c'n put *any* kind of seed in this garden—'fore you know it you got somethin' to eat'" (p. 88). But Moody believes that farming is a difficult and ineffectual way to make a living, especially when there are so many opportunities awaiting her out in the world. Dismissing this way of life, Moody disowns her mother's most sacred investments. The spiritual triumverate of church, earth, and maternal nurturance becomes, for Moody, an inadequate source of self-sufficiency, power, and fertility. Stubbornly, she shuts her ears to her mother's lectures on the pleasures of farming, just as after her baptism her ears are shut to the jubilant shouts of the crowd. Literally as well as figuratively, Moody refuses the voices of past tradition; what beckons her is a voice inside calling her forward across the threshold from the old life to the quest.

Clearly, Moody's consciousness is already more firmly grounded in the public sphere of racial and economic struggle than in her mother's private realm of spiritual compensation. Self-discovery through the toils of farming or righteous obedience to a paternalistic God only serves, Moody realizes, as a pacifier in the face of political impotence, a displacement of her desire to confront social ills. Sondra O'Neale has remarked that, with very few exceptions, the black woman in African American literature has not been concerned with self-discovery. "Her problem usually is more to find a compatible world in which to exist," O'Neale writes.[10] Thus, Anne Moody's quest for personal growth and spiritual wholeness cannot take place outside the context of a social quest to make the world a place where a black woman's identity means something. What makes Moody a hero is her determination to *make* that "compatible world" a reality in this world. Her political future must be made viable before personal identity can develop and thrive.

In this sense, Moody's awakening to her roots in social responsibility corroborates the assumption that women's awareness of the powers of being may be awakened as forcefully through social or political movements as through nature. Moody's quest, grounded in the civil rights movement, confirms that "great powers are revealed through such movements and that the quests for truth or justice or being which they embody are rooted in the powers of being."[11] The quest to renew society thus does not supplant but necessarily precedes her quest for self-realization.

A recurrent motif in African American literature is the black subject's invisibility in white society. Moody's quest constitutes, in this regard, a journey from invisibility to visibility as well as a journey from her own experience of blindness to vision. Working as a domestic for white families, Moody experiences the negation of identity that has traditionally relegated black domestics to the anonymous, silent role of "the maid" in white culture's terms. According to Trudier Harris, the employment of black women as domestics in white families generates the physical and psychological limitations of space that circumscribe black identity. Rather than determining to set her own boundaries in relation to white culture, the black woman who enters the white household as a domestic "initiates compromise." Required to play the stereotypical role of "the maid," the black woman is masked, as her uniform suggests. "Her primary function is to serve the needs of the white family which has thus defined her."[12]

Moody departs from the conventional image of the black domestic in her refusal to sacrifice her identity or her pride to the whites who employ her. Although some of her employers treat her with kindness and respect, she is nevertheless aware at all times of her potential role in the perpetuation of sexual, racial, and economic domination that underlies the relationship between white "master" and black "servant." Although she considers Linda Jean Jenkins a friend and is never challenged for addressing her by her first name, the demoralizing difference behind the common gestures of equality and sensitivity is inevitably revealed when Linda Jean hands over her salary. "I never thought about our color difference when I was with her, except when she paid me," Moody writes. "Only then was I reminded that I was her maid" (p. 93). Thus, it is not in the spiritual exchange but in the material exchange that Moody experiences herself as essentially stripped of spirit, an exploited commodity on the social market.

When Moody begins working for Mrs. Burke, an angry, bitter racist who takes every opportunity to teach Moody lessons in white supremacy, Moody's pride is sparked: she draws her own boundaries. Defiant against Mrs. Burke's imposition, she insists on entering the Burke house through the front door instead of walking around to the back. When asked her opinion, she speaks strongly in favor of school integration although she knows Mrs. Burke is opposed to it. When Mrs. Burke laments the fact that her son needs tutoring in mathematics, Moody unreservedly lets her know that she is considered the best student in her algebra class.

Reluctantly, Mrs. Burke appoints Moody as her son's tutor. In addition, she hires Moody's younger brother, Junior, to do some yard work. Subsequently, with both Moody children working at the house, Mrs. Burke notices some money missing from her purse and accuses Junior of stealing. Harris has pointed out that such politically determined accusations generally reveal more about the white employer's fear of retaliation for prejudice than the black worker's inclination to thievery. "An accusation of theft from the white mistress presupposes her awareness of some injustice in the relationship. . . ."[13] Mrs. Burke's recognition of injustice is revealed to Moody when she is confronted with the accusation against her brother. Moody recalls, "I didn't say anything to her. I walked past her and out of that house for good. And I hoped as time passed I could put not only Mrs. Burke but all her kind out of my life for good" (p. 158).

Moody's emergent sense of self and her new orientation toward the world is emphasized in her growing sense that she is "different" in some significant respect, an outsider even within her own family and community. This vague understanding of her own specialness underscores her candidacy for the heroic quest. A straight-A student, a top athlete, an achiever at everything she undertakes, Moody acknowledges with both pride and discomfort the admiration she elicits from both blacks and whites. Almost in spite of her desire, she senses that she must leave her community in order to fully comprehend her relation to it. Her "election" to a great purpose beyond Centreville is foreshadowed in the account of Moody's election as her high school's homecoming queen—an honor which takes her completely by surprise since she had never considered herself physically attractive.

This incident plays against the common notion that female protagonists derive a sense of power through their physical beauty. For black women this source of power has been socially circumscribed by white standards of feminine beauty that discriminate against black women's skin color and features. "In almost every novel or autobiography written by a black woman," laments Washington, "there is at least one incident in which the dark-skinned girl wishes to be either white or light-skinned with 'good' hair."[14] However, in Moody's memoirs, there are no such incidents. The pride Moody takes in her looks and in her blackness challenges the opinion that black women take no interest in their physical appearance apart from aspiring to look like white women. The pleasure Moody takes in her emergent beauty inspires her confidence but also her anger at the way white men respond to her: "Whenever I was in town white men would stare me into the ground. . . . Mama said to me, 'They think every Negro woman in Centreville who looks like anything should lick their ass and whore around with them.' She warned me that I must never be caught in town after dark alone, and if I was ever approached by white men again, I should walk right past them like I was deaf and blind" (p. 184). Moody's mother, in other words, encourages her daughter to remain voiceless and passive, insensible to the demoralization of her self. Her mother's cautionary belief that a black woman must hide herself and her self-pride from white men indicates the tyranny of the myth of the "wanton" or sexually inexhaustible black "savage." According to Gerda Lerner, this myth assumed that "all black women were eager for sexual exploits . . . and, therefore, deserved none of the consideration and respect granted to white women."[15] And it is not only the white men of Centreville who deny her this respect. Mr. Hicks, her basketball coach, begins to make passes at her during basketball practice. As her body matures, Moody feels tension even at home in the presence of Raymond, her mother's live-in boyfriend. His obvious sexual frustration and desperate sidelong glances finally impel Moody to leave home for good. Recognizing that she is an object not only to the white women of Centreville but to white and black men, she lights out for new territories.

However, on the occasion of the homecoming parade through the center of town, Moody sits atop her float on display before all the people of her community, white and black. Commanding the admiration of the crowd, she feels that she is, indeed, a beautiful sight. Still, she cannot separate this feeling from her consciousness of race. Moody's moment of glory nevertheless "treads upon a world in which the white woman is 'queen.'"[16] When Linda Jean Jenkins regards Moody from the street below, staring up at her with amazement and disbelief, Moody is overcome with desire to affirm her entitlement. "Yes . . . it's me," she longs to say. "Negroes can be beautiful too" (p. 108).

But another eruption diverts her attention. The high school band begins to play "Swanee River." Suddenly, Anne becomes acutely conscious of the black and white faces in the crowd, all singing along, rapt, visibly moved by intense emotion, the implications of which send a chill up her spine. All at once Moody is eaten up with fear as she struggles to interpret the meaning of the expressions passing before her: "The faces of the whites had written on them some strange yearning. The Negroes looked sad. . . . The feeling that the song conveyed stayed with me all evening, and I was cold. That night, when I was crowned Homecoming Queen during half time of the football game, I felt even colder. . . . like I was coming down with something" (p. 109).

Her textualization of the faces of the whites marks Moody's initiation into political literacy. Suddenly, while in the midst of participating in a seemingly innocent ritual of American youth and community spirit, she understands with unwavering certainty that there is no real home for her to come to in this scene. What she reads between the lines of "Swanee River" is a historical text that indicates, for her and her race, a nightmare. Moody's awareness of the death-like transformation taking place inside her parallels the transformation that is about to revolutionize Mississippi.

Moody's involvement with the NAACP and the voter registration drive begins when she is attending college at Tougaloo in Jackson. Her political awakening corresponds with the peeling away of the mask society has imposed on her development. As her commitment to the movement becomes stronger, Stephen Butterfield notes, "episode by episode, she is stripped of her innocence, faith, and above all, her obedient trust of white authority."[17] What is gradually revealed through this process of uncovering is a seed of Emersonian self-reliance. Protesting segregation in the "Whites Only" section of bus stations, staging sit-ins at the lunch counter at Woolworth, Moody moves closer toward the core of inner strength through her deepening connection to the movement against racism. The demonstrations in which she participates, the threats she receives from anti–civil rights activists, and the isolation she endures from family and the nonparticipating black community constitute the necessary trials of her development. Moody's experiences within the movement, her coming of age within the fight against racism, establishes a powerful metaphor for the often violent quest to free the psyche oppressed by societal conventions and the denial of territory based on distinctions of race, gender, or class.

The frontier that Moody's autobiography explores is the territory of her own unacknowledged and unclaimed rage against white society. This is the territory denied her by racist America, a territory that historical forces have worked to condemn and blockade. Moody's quest is to open the doors to this region and affirm her anger as a necessary step in the process of self-affirmation. Her journey may be read not only as a rite of passage but as her right of claiming the explosive tumult within; Moody's experience confirms the fact that neither she nor her anger toward whites is the enemy of her quest. The antagonists are those political and spiritual forces that sanctify the righteousness of passivity or prayer over the righteousness of rage. Her enemy is that which encourages blacks to swallow their indignation. The creature that must be destroyed is the beast within that conditions blacks to repress their bitterness and accept their lots as inferior and unchangeable.

"Anger is better," writes Toni Morrison. "There is a sense of being in anger. A reality and a presence. An awareness of worth." [18] Rather than contain her anger as her mother had done, or release it on her own family as her father had done, Moody's quest takes her in search of an appropriate expression of a powerful will to transform society to suit *her* vision of a freer, stronger black America. Staking claim to her anger becomes the pioneering venture through which the individual spirit may be granted new life. Embracing her anger, Moody has a sense of herself as an active, self-determined subject rather than a passive object of racism. When she hears of the murder of Samuel Quinn, she admits: "I thought of waging a war against the killings all by myself, if no one else would help. I wanted to take my savings, buy a machine gun, and walk down the main street in Centreville cutting down every white person I saw. Then, realizing that I didn't have it in me to kill, I slowly began to escape within myself again" (p. 187).

Moving from invisibility to visibility, Moody engages a dialectic between a desire to withdraw into the self and an equally strong desire to act out destructive, aggressive demonstrations of internalized violence. As the autobiographical narrative leads her from obscurity to the public eye, her anger becomes a concrete force. In this way, *Coming of Age in Mississippi* fully embraces the interconnectedness of psychic and social questing. This dialectic reflects the fundamental politics of Moody's quest, the dynamic interplay of powers manifested both externally in society and internally within the heroic subject herself. Throughout the narrative, Moody moves back and forth between these spheres, always searching for the relationship between external and internal life, public reform and personal form. "Something happened to me as I got more and more involved in the Movement . . . ," she writes. "I had found something outside myself that gave meaning to my life" (p. 263). Understanding this relationship as that which necessarily impels the quest to genuine self-discovery is the task of Moody's "emergent" woman, a woman who "is called to life by the civil rights movement."[19]

Moody's call to life culminates in such a moment of radical awakening to her own powers of being. This discovery constitutes her reclamation of the Holy Grail, a reunion with a lost essence within that anticipates the moment of self-discovery expressed in Ntozake Shange's *colored girls:* "i found God in myself/ and i loved her/ i loved her fiercely."[20]

Indeed, the pattern of Moody's development may be summarized as a journey toward discovering the God within herself; this reclamation of the lost powers of being is a vital theme of the feminized quest, for it establishes a relationship to ultimate powers based on equality and sameness rather than subordination and separation. Moody's quest demands that she abandon faith in the white, paternalistic image of God and reclaim her own powers, in her own image. In order to give birth to this God within herself, this God who *is* herself, Moody must first kill the oppressive God that has remained external to her being. The events of *Coming of Age in Mississippi* move her toward this radical affirmation of a God who is militant and active, a God who will fight rather than dream. Moody's spiritual rebirth is symbolized in the exchange that transforms the very meaning of God into an affirmation of action, anger, and attack against racism. In the key passage of the text, this exchange occurs after Moody hears of the Birmingham church bombing. Overcome with despair and disbelief, she decides that no God truly on the side of righteousness could allow such a thing to happen. After hearing radio reports of the bombing, Moody escapes from the Freedom House and runs toward the woods in search of some familiar comfort in the company of nature: "Before, the woods had always done so much for me. Once I could actually go out into the woods and communicate with God or Nature or something. Now that something didn't come through. . . . More than ever I began to wonder if God actually existed. Maybe God changed as the individual changed, or perhaps grew as one grew. . . . It seemed to me now that there must be two gods, many gods, or no god at all" (pp. 338–339).

In order to locate a source of strength, Moody realizes, she must repudiate all that is external to the purpose of her quest. If, indeed, God changed with the individual, then apparently her hard work had changed nothing; if God grew as the individual grew, then blacks were apparently destined to remain children under the jurisdiction of white masters. Finally, Moody accepts that she must abandon her trust in this God that has forgotten her: "I sat there looking up through the trees," she writes, "trying to communicate with God: I'm through with you. Yes, I'm going to put you down. From now on, I am my own God. I am going to live by the rules I set for myself. I'll discard everything I was once taught about you. Then I'll be you. I will be my own God . . ." (p. 318).

Unburdening herself of this God, Moody is, at last, free to love herself and make her own choices regarding the future of the movement. "We've been praying too long," she determines. "Yes, as a race all we've got is a lot of religion. And the white man's got everything else, including all the dynamite" (p. 319). Thus, Moody takes the explosive potential of her race out of its entrapment in God's house and into the streets, bus stations, department stores, and public parks of Mississippi.

According to Lerner, the civil rights movement provided a "spiritual home" to the young men and women who became active in it.

The "spiritual" family Moody discovers working with the Congress of Racial Equality (CORE) does, indeed, provide Moody more support and comfort than her biological family with whom she eventually loses all contact. Her mother and brother and sisters become frightened for her and for themselves as well. They neither write nor accept her letters for fear of assault from anti–civil rights activists or the Ku Klux Klan. When Moody finds herself all alone at her graduation from Tougaloo, with neither friends nor family in attendance, she finally realizes the extent to which her quest has, ironically, isolated her from the very people for whom she risks her life every day working for CORE. She admits that she feels "funny—sort of like an orphan" (p. 378). Divorced from family, God, and nature, Moody finds herself truly orphaned, bereft of all familiar ties. These issues of abandonment, departure, and renewed spiritual rebirth through the movement are central to Moody's personal and narrative development; they constitute the central themes of the memoir, an autobiographical journey that attempts to capture a period of continuous motion and tumultuous emergence into new territories.

From Centreville to New Orleans, from one-room shack to college dorm, from domestic work to NAACP outposts, Moody remains throughout the better part of the text very much in motion. "The movement" itself is the name accorded a new kind of life for her, a new family and a new home paradoxically rooted in the external world of public events and politics. However, unlike the classic male quest of Campbell's monomyth, there is no return to the old community for Moody. Moody's relationships within the movement and her new self-orientation constitute both a new home in the world and a new world in herself.

Through the trials of the quest, Moody learns not only to doubt her reliance upon white society but her reliance upon the movement itself. *Coming of Age in Mississippi* ends with Moody "on the road" in a bus filled with civil rights activists heading to Washington, D.C., for the 1963 Freedom March. In the final passage of *Coming of Age in Mississippi*, beneath the chant of optimistic freedom riders singing "We Shall Overcome," Moody is uncertain whether they will really ever accomplish their goal of freedom. "I wonder. I really wonder," she concludes. But in spite of her doubts, Anne Moody's *Coming of Age in Mississippi* ends with the promise of continued growth and motion—not just the physical motion of the bus driving the freedom riders forward but Moody's intellectual activity as she relentlessly questions and examines her own processes, demonstrating self-possession, a capacity to continue moving, thinking, and fighting for what she believes in, even if it means continuing without the support of a "movement" behind her.

As *Coming of Age in Mississippi* ends, its subject is, indeed, going somewhere. But where, exactly, remains uncertain. Her narrative concludes with a question rather than an answer; however, the uncertain goal of the quest suggests that its movement, like "the movement," must continue to evolve, as Moody herself must continue to move and keep her eyes fixed on whatever lies ahead. In a sense, then, future movements are implied to begin where the autobiography ends: her twenty-year journey toward the freedom rally in Washington *has*, in fact, opened the door for a new definition of heroism based on woman's spiritual and social emergence. Moody's feminization of the quest is postulated upon the historical politicization of race relations and the female subject.

While literary critics have tended to look for the source of sorrow and weakness in the lives of black female protagonists, Sondra O'Neale believes it essential that contemporary critics "approach the 'new' black women's literature . . . to see if it has indeed revealed those *strengths* that have made possible the black woman's survival."[21] Anne Moody's autobiography not only reveals these strengths but shows how they are developed through the trials of growing up poor, black, and female. Her quest is a courageous act of self-creation which triumphs over stereotypes that have prescribed images of blacks and literary forms that have codified black experience according to the perceptions and priorities of white experience. Scorning dreamers, she dares to awaken a sleeping world to a nightmare she can no longer tolerate. Her eyes remain open, her voice strong, her feet firmly planted on this earth. Finally, *Coming of Age in Mississippi* constructs new patterns and images of heroic action by considering from one woman's vantage point the question of what was gained by the movement. Years later, in "The Civil Rights Movement: What Good Was It?" Alice Walker would answer the question this way: "To know is to exist: to exist is to be involved, to move about, to see the world with my own eyes. This, at least, the Movement has given me."[22]

6. "Happily at Ease in the Dark"

Marilynne Robinson's
Housekeeping

I believe it was the crossing of the bridge that changed me finally. The terrors of the crossing were considerable. Twice I stumbled and fell. And a wind came up from the north, so that the push of the wind and the pull of the current were the same, and it seemed as though they were not to be resisted. And then it was so dark. —ROBINSON, *HOUSEKEEPING*

In "A World of Women: Marilynne Robinson's *Housekeeping*," Elizabeth Meese remarks, "Tradition, as a guide to interpretation, does not easily accommodate or unlock Robinson's *Housekeeping* . . . It is as though [she] sets out to discover the nature of woman distinct from her existence as a male invention."[1] Certainly, *Housekeeping* shares with the most effective feminist writings a commitment to liberating woman, the enigmatic "dark continent," from the arresting "light" of male exploration. Traditionally, American literature has celebrated the primacy of masculine crusades, developmental campaigns coextensive with the pronunciation of female "otherness." In Maureen Ryan's assessment, "The classic American experience is the rejection of the restrictive forces of civilization, represented by female characters like the termagant Dame Van Winkle, Huck's Aunt Sally, and Tom Wingfield's suffocating mother and sister."[2] However, along with its refusal of categorical "otherness" as woman's literary destiny, *Housekeeping* transforms the "lighting out" motif traditionally reserved for male protagonists into a feminized quest toward a self-naming, or self-mapping, of the female questing ground.

In this sense, Marilynne Robinson's novel portrays a dissident daughter, an initiate on a quest for new literary forms and themes that would enable an understanding of women's lives. *Housekeeping* is a novel born of a transformative vision of the past, and as such it is a novel deeply concerned with the dual processes of avoiding entrapment in traditional narrative structures and discovering an authentic capacity to name and validate female experience.

This uncharted, feminized experience is revealed in a place inhabited by loss—loss of tradition, of participation in history, and especially loss of the mother, whose absence makes "any present moment most significant for what it does not contain."[3] As Ruth, the adolescent narrator, explores the territory of woman's absence she discovers a frontier not limited by the arbitrary boundaries of home, community, and inheritance, but a secret world beyond the static order of housekeeping, a world navigable only by way of dislocation and breach of phallocentric conceptual and symbolic order. "Transcendence," writes Annis Pratt, "necessitates passing through and beyond sexual politics to a new environment, a new kind of space."[4] Ruth's adoption of a transient's life confirms this rite of passage. Her choice of vagrants and drifters as proper role models affirms her participation in the quest to explore this "new kind of space."

Still, it is possible to read Robinson's *Housekeeping* within a more familiar frame, for the novel works within two conventional American literary motifs: the quest-romance, or initiation story, and the "on the road" saga. In *Housekeeping*, these major themes of the paradigmatic male quest plot are transformed into a female vision that sees a capacity for autonomous self-definition as well as a capacity for nurturance in women's lives. Through a reworking of the "lighting out" motif that invokes elements of feminist literary and psychoanalytic theory, Robinson's novel explores new images of female selfhood and new modes of female social involvement.

At the novel's conclusion, Ruth is initiated into a life of apparently ceaseless drifting with her Aunt Sylvie, a dedicated vagrant. Like Sylvie, Ruth accepts female identity as never fixed, never captured, but a self composed of many selves, alive in multiplicity, always in motion. This commitment to a self in flight from reification supports an essential social quest as well; rather than withdraw into spiritual isolation, death, or madness, Ruth and Sylvie enact their renunciation of the common world *within* that world. By ritualizing a refusal of gender expectations they transform the quest into a public drama of rejection and renewal, a call for radical cultural change.

"If I had the choice," Ruth admits, "I would work in a truck stop. I like to overhear the stories strangers tell each other . . ." (p. 214). From an objective distance, Ruth finds comfort in observing strangers drawn together by familiar narrative structures that allow their lives to intersect, however briefly. These narrative strategies are of no use to her, however, for they claim the power to absorb her into inappropriate patterns, like the newspaper headline—"LAKE CLAIMS TWO"—which erroneously reports that Ruth and Sylvie are dead, absorbed by the dark depths of the lake. Inaccurate reports of female possibility subsume the meaning of Ruth's silence into the culturally expected categories of female need and behavior. "What have I to do with these ceremonies of sustenance, of nurturing?" Ruth asks. "They begin to ask why I do not eat anything myself. Once they begin to look at me like this, it is best that I leave" (p. 214).

The final sentence of Ihab Hassan's *Radical Innocence* proclaims, "The curse of Columbus is still with us: every one must rediscover America for himself—alone."[5] In *Housekeeping* Ruth and Sylvie's dispossession from the male legacy of isolated heroism enables them to share a destiny of mutual heroic agency and female solidarity. Their commitment to one another both defies the conditions of the male questing pattern and redefines the notion of human agency to include relational capacity. As Roberta Rubenstein usefully points out, in choosing a path together, rather than separate lives of solitary wandering, Ruth and Sylvie become heroic "neither through the accoutrements of their gender nor through relationships with men but rather through a strong nurturant and reciprocal female bond." *Housekeeping* asserts itself as a radical text, Rubenstein further suggests, "in its implication that the establishment of female selfhood . . . need not be conceived in terms of a solitary heroic journey or an erotic union."[6] By enacting a quest that is both personal and social, both internally and externally effective, Ruth and Sylvie transcend psychic entrapment in what Jean Stafford called "the interior castle of the mind." As a representative of the new female questing protagonist in American fiction, Ruth runs in relation to yet independently of the nurturing domestic ties that the feminized quest

transforms. In this way, she discovers new inclusive territories for
female development and the representation of female experience in
American literature.

At the novel's opening there is a declaration, an act of self-naming
that consciously acknowledges and subverts the traditionally exclusive field of male literary authority: "My name is Ruth." The reinvention of Melville's Ishmael wrests power from the father's sphere
and affirms identity in a voice that is at once distinctly American and
distinctly female.[7] At the core of this identity, however, there is a
question: "When did I become so unlike other people?" (p. 214).
This is the mystery Ruth seeks to resolve through memory. The territory of the past is symbolized in the relentless force and depth of
Fingerbone lake. The lake is only part of a pattern of metaphor established in the text that aligns houses, bodies of water, and
women's bodies as impermanent receptacles of human essence,
spirit, history. And history unfolds as the sum of the many stories
women tell about their lives.

Housekeeping is similarly framed by a central narrative, the very
substance of which is a gathering of fragments, dreams, snapshots,
anecdotes, and old newspaper articles pressed between the yellowed
pages of dusty almanacs. Robinson's accumulative breadth of allusion and relation creates a ripple effect like the residual undulations
of water emanating from the shattered surface of Fingerbone lake
when the train carrying Ruth's grandfather plunged off the bridge
and was lost. This is how history works in *Housekeeping*: a moment
shatters the glassy surface, and all the future is an echo or an undu-
lation that one can always trace back to an accident, a disappearance, a dropped stitch in the woven fabric of time.

Even the name of the town itself, Fingerbone, suggests this fragile, fragmentary quality. The name reminds us that each moment of a
life and each story recalled from the past is—like a single point on
the map or the tiniest joint of the hand—but one small piece of
a whole. Ruth's question—"When did I become so unlike other
people?"—impels this effort to restore these fragments into a coherent form. "What are these fragments for, if not to be knit up finally?" she asks (p. 92). Somehow, if all these gestures of the hand
can be comprehended, all these missing buttons replaced and lost
socks restored, we can recall the coherent past, become the whole
subject, and stave off the threat of difference. And, indeed, the fem-

inized quest is a response to the difficulty of recognizing and coming
to terms with difference. The "lighting out" experience in *Housekeeping* is thus an experience among the fragments, a time of collecting whatever moments our histories have left scattered. Ruth's rite of
passage, up until the point of her call to adventure, is an explanatory
struggle to impose order on pieces that she cannot fit into the town's
prescribed symbolic and conceptual logic.

These moments and pieces that are swept up in the course of
Housekeeping haunt the very consciousness of the novel in the same
way that the memory of the great train derailment haunts the inhabi-
tants of Fingerbone and the Foster women especially. This accident
provides a dominant metaphor for sustaining the narrative's gradual
motion into depth and darkness. As the story is told, no one in Fingerbone actually witnessed the train wreck, no one saw it happen.
Bits of speculation and lies are gradually woven into an authorized
history of the event. The Fireball was halfway across the bridge
when the engine derailed and pulled the rest of the train over and
down to the bottom of the lake. Ruth's account of the accident pre-
figures the design of her narrative: "Memory is the sense of loss,"
she says, "and loss pulls us after it. God himself was pulled after us
into the vortex we made when we fell, or so the story goes" (p. 194).
"What both haunts and fascinates the townspeople of Fingerbone is
an extraordinary disappearance, a deception designed to bridge the
darkness, and, finally, the absence of memory in our effort to fully
account for that deception; for what are all these facts and fragments
if not only imperfections of darkness?

By becoming a drifter, Ruth fulfills her grandmother's belief that
life was "a road down which one traveled, an easy enough road
through a broad country, and that one's destination was there from
the very beginning." (p. 9). Her prophecy recalls Faulkner's Lena
Grove, a vagrant in her own right, walking barefoot and pregnant in
her mail-order dress toward Doanes Mill. Robinson, however, betrays no allegiance to female models of fertility, nor do her women
"light out" in search of men. The women of *Housekeeping* determine
their own destinies, and the world they inhabit is, indeed, a world of
women—like the convent in Mary McCarthy's *Memories of a Catholic Girlhood*—a world in which conventional relationships with men
as husbands or fathers seem not to exist at all. Men occupy a place
primarily in the "indifferent" past, expressionless faces staring out

of newsreel footage. Only the sheriff, who represents the watchful, disproving threat of male law, comes across as a living measure of the distance between the life Sylvie and Ruth share together and the life of the community around them. The sheriff in this context, however, represents not so much an annihilating agent as the degree of fear that Sylvie's housekeeping induces among the townspeople. As Meese writes, "In a sense, one of the text's ultimate purposes is to explicate difference as represented by Sylvie's transiency—a way of life Fingerbone children are taught to fear so that their souls remain captives of ordinary society."[8]

Transience is a truth that tortures the captive soul with the force of irresolvable paradox. For the essence of paradox is impermanence, a constant dislocation and restoration. As Ruth phrases it, "The sorrow is that every soul is put out of house" (p. 179). This is the essence of *Housekeeping*, that what is lost will become extraordinary by its absence, and this is itself a kind of freedom. *Housekeeping* is an articulation of essence freed from captivity, children freed from society, women freed from houses. What makes Sylvie an eyesore for the residents of Fingerbone is that her housekeeping openly acknowledges the paradox that women are the captives rather than the keepers of house. What makes her an unfit parent is her tendency to disregard or otherwise undo the boundaries of home. Doors and windows are left open. Leaves and scraps of litter gather in the corners and niches of the living room. "We had crickets in the pantry, squirrels in the eaves, sparrows in the attic . . . Everytime a door was opened anywhere in the house there was a sound from all the corners of lifting and alighting . . . Thus finely did our house become attuned to the orchard and to the particularities of weather" (p. 85).

Sylvie engages in no struggle against the inevitable exchange of the values of indoors and outdoors. The boundaries of her house are kept permeable, yielding. In this sense, Sylvie's housekeeping corroborates the flexibility and fluidity of ego boundaries that feminist theorists such as Gilligan suggest illuminate the importance of relationship in women's lives. In the Foster house, the external world blends with the interior sanctity of home. Sylvie embraces the essences and elements that housekeeping should, by common definition, remove and disinfect. Says Ruth, "Sylvie in a house was more or less like a mermaid in a ship's cabin. She preferred it sunk in the very element it was meant to exclude" (p. 9).

As Ruth individuates and gradually sees herself as excluded from the very world she is meant to inhabit, she comes to identify herself with Sylvie's kind of existence. With Sylvie's guidance, she conceives of an open, expansive territory that corresponds with her notion of a self. As her sister Lucille yearns to participate in social "reality" and embraces conventional images of and expectations for female character, Ruth becomes even more confident in her belief that she belongs with Sylvie, apart from the ordinary world that Lucille accepts. This world offers Ruth nothing except a future of entrapment and inertia. "For it seemed to me that nothing I had lost, or might lose, could be found there, or to put it another way, it seemed that something I had lost might be found in Sylvie's house" (pp. 123–124). And, indeed, what she finds in Sylvie's house is that element never conceived of as relevant in a sheltering home: a dynamic relationship to the outside world, a necessary voyage to search out one's capacity for grace and comfort in the darkness. Even as a small child, Ruth recognizes her ability to merge with the outside. Once afraid of the dark, she is told by her grandmother to close her eyes so she would not see it. Ruth recalls, "That was when I noticed the correspondence between the space within the circle of my skull and the space around me" (p. 198).

Robinson develops this correspondence, along with a number of others important to the text, by accumulating images that resonate with increasing force as the moments of Ruth's narrative unfold. Her highly allusive and poetic language works to undo contrasts and oppositions, so that gradually Ruth's awakening to difference transcends the ordinary tension of the binary and gives way to a harmonious resolution of inside/outside, dark/light, presence/absence. This preoccupation with corresponding contrasts informs the eventual breaking apart of the two sisters, Ruth and Lucille. At first, Ruth is able to refer to them as one consciousness. But gradually the world begins to draw them into different spaces and begins to shape them according to the adult roles each will assume. "I myself," says Ruth, "felt the gaze of the world as a distorting mirror that squashed her plump and stretched me narrow" (p. 9). Thus, while Lucille acquires a maternal width and roundness, Ruth acquires the length of road. Ruth and Lucille thus literally embody two opposing possibilities, intimacy and distance, possibilities that can be traced nevertheless to a shared origin, Helen, their mother. But the girls carry

very different images of their mother, an indication that the vacant
territories of Ruth and Lucille will require of each a different kind of
journey. Lucille's Helen was "orderly, vigorous, and sensible," a
brown-haired widow who was killed in an accident. Ruth's Helen
was a redhead who tended her children with a "gentle indifference
that made [Ruth] feel she would have liked to have been even more
alone" (p. 109). She was an "abandoner" whose husband had abandoned her and whose death was well known to have been a suicide.

Ruth and Lucille diverge most dramatically in their separate reactions to Sylvie's housekeeping. "I was content with Sylvie," says
Ruth, "so it was a surprise to me when I realized that Lucille had
begun to regard other people with the calm, horizontal look of settled
purpose with which, from a slowly sinking boat, she might have regarded a not-too-distant shore" (p. 92). Subsequently, Lucille makes
a bid for what she perceives to be the normal adolescent experience;
she cultivates an interest in friends and clothing, sets her hair in
rollers, and attends school dances. Ruth, too, undergoes some of the
typical growing pains and crises common to girls her age. She names
herself a loner and a dreamer. Her unusual height, which she fears
is totally out of control, likens her image to that of the "adolescent
grotesque" which Annis Pratt defines as an archetype of women's fiction. Like most adolescents, she experiences herself as ungainly and
invisible; and yet, unlike Molly Fawcett, she wages no rebellion
against the unwelcoming world. And unlike the young Mary McCarthy, she feels no desire to be noticed by the society surrounding her.
"I modeled my indifference on Sylvie's," she explains. When Lucille
moves out of Sylvie's house to live with her high school home eco-
nomics teacher, who represents the very antithesis to Sylvie's domestic engineering, Ruth feels again the darkness of absence and
loss calling her out into Sylvie's world. Ruth and Lucille resign
themselves solemnly to the fact that, although they share a biological
origin, this alone will not determine their destinies. "I had no sister
after that . . . ," says Ruth; and yet Lucille's absence makes her
enormous in Ruth's consciousness in a way that she could never
have been while in Ruth's company. The novel's final image is of
Lucille, as Ruth imagines her years later, her thoughts taken over by
what they do not contain. And who could know, asks Ruth, "how she
does not watch, does not wait, does not listen, does not hope, and
always for me and Sylvie" (p. 219).

Again, the dramatic rebirth, or second birth, defined by Carol Christ as an essential stage in women's quests, is represented. In *Housekeeping* this symbolic ritual of transformation and renewal is enacted during the course of Ruth's overnight trip to the lake with Sylvie. On their way out to the lake Ruth feels a powerful sense of symbiotic union with Sylvie as she nestles herself into the folds of her coat. "We were the same . . . I crowded and slept in her very shape like an unborn child" (p. 145). In a stolen rowboat, Sylvie takes Ruth out to a broad point on the lake where she knows of a fallen house that she tells Ruth is inhabited by feral children. Here Robinson merges the natural landscape with the yielding, fecund body of the mother; together, Sylvie and Ruth ascend the soft cleavage between two close mountains of pink rock. Yet to Ruth this region appears chaotic, ravaged. The mountains are too close together, suffocating. When Ruth turns to find Sylvie suddenly vanished, she reexperiences the trauma of her abandonment and comes to terms with the impermanence of all houses, all flesh and relationship, and she sees that in a way she has at last reclaimed her loss. Longing itself, she realizes, empowers and impels the spirit perpetually forward toward the past. Or as Ruth phrases it, "To crave and to have are as like as a thing and its shadow . . . For to wish for a hand on one's hair is all but to feel it. So whatever we may lose, very craving gives it back to us again" (pp. 152–153).

Ruth destroys the cellar door of the cabin. She begins tearing at loose planks with violent energy, for she no longer believes that the house contains children. The action dramatically symbolizes Ruth's aggressive action in the face of entrapment and boundaries. It declares a radical rebellion of female spirit against the literary fixtures and cultural barriers that would deny her the imaginative and social mobility to rediscover herself. No children live in this house, Ruth realizes, for there is nothing to live for at home except, perhaps, an illusion of absolute warmth, an illusion of absolute light, and an illusory faith in the power of fragments to sustain such absoluteness. "It is better to have nothing," realizes Ruth, "for at last even our bones will fall. It is better to have nothing" (p. 159). This is the moment of Ruth's awakening to power, symbolized in an act of destruction. For to declare oneself free is inevitably to destroy, or as Ruth puts it, "to break the tethers of need." "The only true birth," she says, "would be a final one, which would free us from watery darkness" (p. 162). Ultimately, our final birth, and the quest that leads us to it, may be likened to a kind of death. The questing drama tears the lid off the image of one's former self and propels the essential powers of being away from social labeling into the truth of transience.

Ruth's symbolic second birth takes place during the return voyage across the lake with Sylvie; however, the moment is not explicated through direct action but rather suggested through a brilliant accumulation of images and metaphors. "Sylvie climbed in and settled herself with a foot on either side of me," Ruth describes. "She twisted around and pushed us off with an oar, and then she began to reach and pull, reach and pull . . . I lay like a seed in a husk. The immense water thunked and thudded beneath my head" (pp. 161–162). This scene recalls an earlier description of Ruth heading out to the point with Sylvie. Here she crawled "under her body and out between her legs" (p. 146). Clearly, what Robinson wants to legitimize in these passages is woman's potential to be reborn in a ritual predicated on self-awareness, a ritual that transcends the agency of the mother's body and empowers the agency of the self.

At the conclusion of these episodes, it becomes apparent to Ruth that the journey has been staged by Sylvie as part of her education and induction into vagrancy. This "richness of grace" Ruth feels has been bestowed upon her like the gift of an enveloping coat. Thus, Ruth is awakened not only to the truth of transience, but to the privilege of having been granted light in the darkness. This light confirms in Ruth a destiny, an ability both to negotiate the dark on her own and to cleave to Sylvie as once the biblical Ruth cleaved, fully self-aware, to her mother-in-law, Naomi. In this sense, Robinson's novel confirms Joanne Frye's assertion that women's stories, like women's lives, "can have multiple centers." And along with this multiplicity comes the possibility of developing "alternative thematic unities based on female autonomy and informed by female experience."[9] These alternatives should remind women not only that they are independent but that they are united in the struggle to assert this independence, culturally and textually.

In *The Poetics of Reverie: Childhood, Language, and the Cosmos*, Gaston Bachelard tranforms the quest to unite past and present consciousness into a language of fire that lights images of psychic discovery and rebirth. "There are childhood reveries that surge forth with the brilliance of a fire. The poet finds his childhood again by telling it with a tone (*verbe*) of fire."[10] In *Housekeeping* the lighting of Psyche's torch is represented by the fires that Sylvie and Ruth set shortly before their escape across the railroad bridge over Fingerbone lake. In Apuleius's tale, Psyche's lighting of the torch and her discovery of the true identity of her lover marks the loss of Eros and the beginning of her voyage to reclaim female power.

In *Housekeeping* the symbolic burning of the Foster house and the bonfire of books and magazines that Sylvie tends in the backyard signal Ruth's ritual initiation into darkness. Fire gives rise to vision and illuminates the moment of dispossession. The charred, abandoned Foster house suggests the abandoned womb of the mother's body as Ruth prepares to be ceaselessly reborn through transience. By destroying all illusions of security and enclosure, Sylvie enables Ruth's recognition of the fragile forces which have held her, and the townspeople of Fingerbone, for so long in one place. Watching as the bonfire burns, as the pages of magazines turn to cinders and spiral up in the air, Ruth reflects: "It had never occurred to me that words, too, must be salvaged, though when I thought about it, it seemed obvious. It was absurd to think things were held in place, are held in place, by a web of words" (p. 200). To "light out" is to no longer be held in place by this web of language, to spiral upward with the spark of fire, to transform the page written upon. Robinson's novel grants motion to the words that would otherwise keep women stationary, fixing them eternally as daughters, mothers, wives. Ruth's own narrative awareness emphasizes her revelation that the wreckage of the past is preserved only through a fragile weaving of language which is ultimately volatile, fragmentary, and dangerously combustible.

Nor Hall defines initiation as "an active entry into darkness." It requires that we enter into "an experience of psychic significance with one's eyes closed, mouth shut, wearing a veil—a kind of veil that paradoxically permits seeing."[11] In *Housekeeping* that "psychic encounter" is expressed through the feminization of the questing theme. To "light out," in terms of woman's experience, is not to shun or tame the darkness but rather to gain the perspective that darkness affords. Only thus can we understand that *women are* the dark world, and when they run from this world, they run from themselves, their visions. "When one looks from darkness into light," says Ruth, "one sees all the difference between here and there" (p. 158). The difference, indeed, is the discovery that a woman's quest—unlike the classic male quest—is not measurable by any resolution reached, grail attained, or dark region overcome. Nor is it measurable by time, a reconciliation with the shadows of the past. A woman's quest is a revolution—a historical and psychological revolution—set into motion by the recognition of a missing person: herself.

♋

Finally, *Housekeeping* offers more than a feminist alternative to the Huck Finns and Sal Paradises of American fiction: the novel is a powerful celebration of women's collective history and memory, which also recognizes the fact that women are of vastly different origins, on various paths toward various goals. A shared understanding of our lives as women has, very persistently and very rightly, posed difficulties for feminist activists, critics, and theorists in trying to establish a common ground in support of differences in race, class, religion, and sexual orientation. Calling upon the associative powers of myth and both the Old and New Testament, Robinson attempts to achieve a sense of unity among women by reaching beyond the commonly acknowledged barriers that subdivide their political concerns and engagements.

In *Housekeeping* there is a common territory for women to explore: a conceptual territory, a territory in need not only of discovery but of invention. Women have known this open space in other forms: as the gap in their understanding of who they are, the lack of cultural images that empower and affirm a female sense of worth; as the unwritten story that they longed for but never heard or read; as the lost record of their common birth, of some documentation of their experience as women and as individuals. To claim this legacy and to explore it, to collect the scattered images, words, and fragments that we have been able to salvage from the wreckage of the past and from the depth of darkness—this is the purpose of Robinson's *Housekeeping*, and it is the purpose that American and feminist critics can most readily claim as common to us all.

7. Shifting Gears

Mona Simpson's
Anywhere But Here

*The runways of the Bay City Airport were just clearings in the low woods,
rimmed with aspen and pine. When the plane shuddered and rumbled and
bumped, we closed our eyes, clinging. When I opened my hand, a few
moments later, my mother's nails had bitten in so hard there was blood.
We both felt terrified of landing.* —SIMPSON, *ANYWHERE BUT HERE*

In "A Desire of One's Own" Jessica Benjamin achieves radical
reclamation of the female subject by reaching for the root, the essential quest of a still imminent question: "What *does* a woman want?"
Formulating her theories within a feminist psychoanalytic context,
Benjamin suggests that "what is experientially female is the association of desire with a space," a territory in which a woman may discover an authentic female selfhood constituted by her capacity for
both immanence and transcendence, nurturance and autonomy, the
salient forces which dialectically describe woman's primary identification with the maternal parent.[1]

To seek out this territory and challenge the exclusive boundaries
of gendered images and actions is to redefine heroism in terms specific to woman's experience in patriarchal culture. Recognizing at
once the lack of alternative symbols to represent female desire, and
the fact that such symbols—even if they did exist—would, by the
very fact of their participation in the symbolic order, support a cognitive mode that defines itself through the devaluation of the feminine, feminist theorists such as Benjamin have suggested that what
women want are new cognitive strategies, female-specific modes of
representation. The desire to search out and forge new modes of representation is, I believe, informing the emergent theme of the quest
in contemporary women's writing. Female transience, with its cen-

tral image of women "lighting out" from male-defined spaces in
search of new territories of self-discovery, responds not only to the
question of woman's desire but to the quest for a new mode of representing desire within the context of a woman's journey toward self-
understanding.

Mona Simpson's *Anywhere But Here*, a first novel published in
1987, provides a state-of-the-quest report from the field of contemporary women's fiction. The spatial patterns that reflect women's
journeys toward self-definition are expressed in the spaces between
women, spaces that both connect and divide self and other, mother
and daughter. The potential of spatial metaphors to represent
woman's quest is underscored by the transforming image of female
agency with which the novel opens—Adele Diamond and her
daughter, Ann, heading west to California in a stolen Lincoln Continental, lighting out in search of a life together and a life apart.

"Sometimes," says Ann, "it seemed years, it had been known between us, decided, we were going to California. . . . We were running away from family. We'd left home."[2] Portraying mother and
daughter in flight from male-dominant structures that prohibit a miti-
gation of their dependence and the expression of a separate, individuated selfhood, Simpson's novel enacts a dramatic shift in literary convention. By translating the patterns of a classic American
romance with life on the road into a psychic mapping of the intimate
spaces that express the female subject, Simpson creates a fictional
"topoanalysis," the term coined by Gaston Bachelard for the "sys-
tematic psychological study of the sites of our intimate lives."[3]

A novel centrally concerned with the topoanalysis of female desire, *Anywhere But Here* offers a fictional analogue for one of the
questions that feminist psychoanalytic criticism has sought to address through mother-identification theory: "whether the price of
selfhood," for women, is "the loss of the mother's love, or con-
versely, whether the price of love is to be the inhibition of autonomy."[4] With this question guiding the development of her two main
characters, Simpson examines the symbiotic relationship of Ann and
her mother Adele, a woman whose unresolved and unacknowledged
psychic dependency on her own mother, Ida, leads her along a path
of intense and exclusive attachments through which she attempts to
locate a coherent self. En route Adele seeks relentlessly to cathect
with external objects—cars, houses, real estate agents, lovers, her

daughter—all reflections of an absolute inner-space longing to merge with the outside. But finally these objects only serve to exacerbate an inner emptiness that compels Adele to search for something more, something that she once possessed. And just as compulsively as she forms object-relational patterns, she abandons them in an effort to purge herself of longings which threaten to collapse the very institutions and traditions that she needs in order to support herself.

"Strangers almost always love my mother. . . . there's something about her, some romance, some power. She's absolutely herself" (p. 13). Ann's recognition remains accurate not in spite of but precisely because of Adele's wish to be perceived as the absolute object rather than the absolute subject of desire. By asserting her powers of seduction, Adele relentlessly pursues her own longings in the presumed interest of pleasing others. Her quest leads her gradually toward the recognition that one can be *both* the object *and* subject of desire.

Anywhere But Here confronts this paradox as well as the exclusive function of the phallus for representing desire. Simpson's novel centers on a paradoxical situation in the developmental processes of the female child: her only solution to the lack of a symbolic vehicle requires that she set up rigorous boundaries which allow her to abandon the mother to search out a symbol of her own desire. The daughter's seduction by the father and her separation from the mother "represents independence and individuation, progress, activity, and participation in the real world."[5] The path to an individuated adulthood is thus defined as the path that leads women to abandon their mothers. When Adele licks her finger to wipe a smudge of lipstick from her daughter's mouth, Ann runs immediately over to the sink and spits. "I tasted her saliva, it was different from mine." As she begins to recognize difference within the context of such intimacy, Ann realizes, "I wanted to get away from her" (p. 21).

Ann's growing awareness of the mother-daughter bond makes it possible for her to identify Adele's incessant hunger as a longing to restore a missing part of herself, something she might have left at home. During an afternoon visit with Ida and Adele's older sister, Carol, Ann speaks for her mother as if they are one consciousness. She watches Adele stuff herself with homemade pie and feel at once "full and still sure that there [is] not enough." In the company of three generations of mothers and daughters, all greedy for and frightened of the primal bonds they share with one another, Adele becomes restless and saddened by a need for something apparently greater than the pieces of a whole can provide. "She stared at the half pie left in the tin pan," observes Ann. "Carol was always born first. Her mother already had a daughter when she was born" (p. 100).

Adele's narcissistic greed is most powerfully expressed in the deeply conflicted impulses that distort her perceptions of the boundaries between herself and her daughter. The erotic conflict of Adele's desire to merge and Ann's desire to pull away from her mother resonates in the spatial negotiations between mother and daughter as they fight to determine the boundaries of selfhood and the site of female subjectivity.

> She kissed me on the lips and I shirked. When her hand
> reached down to the elastic of my pajama pants, I stiffened and
> bucked away from her. "Don't."
> "I don't know why not," she said . . . "Can't I be proud of
> your little body that I made?" When she stared at me like that,
> it seemed she could take something just by looking. (P. 263)

Rousing her daughter from sleep, Adele pulls the blankets down and whispers in sheer amazement at her own image: "You are a long-limbed beauty. You're my jewel. I have to take you somewhere they can see it" (p. 60). The appropriating gaze of the mother that refuses to recognize the child's separateness illustrates the "psychotic distortion of the normal pre-oedipal relationship," which Chodorow identifies as predominantly a mother-daughter phenomenon.[6] As Ann fights to differentiate and remove herself from the space controlled by her mother's gaze, Adele advances in direct proportion to her daughter's retreat, framing her object more narrowly. "[My mother's] gaze was like a leash as we walked," Ann protests (p. 59). In Simpson's novel, the maternal field of vision is a field fully occupied by paradox, the function of the gaze being not to find its object but its mirrored subject. Thus, the reproduction of mothering is described as a process that falsely empowers the mother's eye/I; however, the novel makes it clear that this viewing subject remains always a split subject, a battlefield. But while Adele's vision of unity is shown to be incapable of supporting a balance of two equally demanding subjects, her dream of television stardom, which she projects onto Ann, sustains Adele's hope of one day experiencing herself absolutely, as the infant experiences its own moment of absoluteness through its contiguous relationship to the mother's holding gaze.

"My mother had given me choices all my life," says Ann, "and I'd never learned to choose. . . . I'd learned a long time ago to pick the things she hadn't picked, the one she didn't want. That way she would get me both, because she couldn't bear to give up what she wanted for me" (p. 91). The gratification of Adele's longings thus become possible only to the extent that she remains in full charge of her daughter's desire.

Ann begins to reproduce this violation with the younger children whom she seduces into the bathroom and whom she challenges to undress so that she can take nude photographs of them. As a reward, Ann tells the children that they will gain initiation into an exclusive club. She assures each child that no one but her will ever see the pictures: slowly, Ann amasses a collection of photographs which she keeps hidden in her bedroom. Through this furtive enterprise, Ann assembles a tribute to childbirth itself, an event that finds all its subjects naked and vulnerable in the grips of an indifferent world—and, indeed, an initiation occurs insofar as Ann recognizes *herself* in this universal dilemma. However, what she also discovers in these secret sessions is the surprising ease with which her "subjects" hand their bodies over to her as objects of her will. "I was always amazed when they did it," she recalls. "People are so easy to boss. . . . It's amazing the power people give you" (pp. 51–52). Ann observes that her male models stare back at the camera, attempting a kind of gritty defiance. But with her first female model—motherless Mary Griling—she discovers an almost limitless power. Through Mary's passivity and unquestioning trust, Ann is shown her own vulnerability in her relationship with Adele. As Ann begins to recognize her capacity to move between the roles of object and subject of desire, these experiments in image reproduction constitute for her both a form of revenge and a form of self-forgiveness; within the limits of the photograph, she is able to contain both empathy and indifference.

"I'd been taught all my life," Ann says, "or I knew somehow . . . that you couldn't trust the kind faces of things, that the world was painted and behind the thin, bright surface was darkness and the only place I was safe was home with my mother. But it seemed safer outside now, safer with indifference than care" (p. 194). As Ann recognizes the destructive force of Adele's mother love, she realizes her potential for transcendence in her ability to derive a balanced nurturance from the outside world, the earth, the sphere of play and imagination. Rolling down a grassy hill, Ann feels the safe embrace of the earth; as Adele drives, Ann places her hand outside the car window and feels "the moving air . . . solid, like a breast" (p. 18). What this image suggests is that female transience enables a reexperience of the mother's body in the arms of the external world; Ann's transcendent strength is an imagination parented by both darkness and light.

Mirroring the shift in thematic pattern, the novel traces a shift in the representation of female subjectivity in the social sphere. *Anywhere But Here* challenges the Oedipal division of maternal and paternal spheres which prescribes cultural conventions and literary images, connecting women to the private, domestic space. The implications of this pervasive pattern have been demonstrated, for example, in Erik Erikson's theory of woman's "natural" predisposition to "inner space" and man's basic adaption to outer space, the sphere of adventure and discovery.[7] Benjamin has explained that by splitting these spheres "two complementary elements that should be held in tension are instead set up as opposites, with one side idealized and the other devalued."[8] In accord with recent feminist theory, Simpson's novel seeks to redefine a relationship between home and the world, polarized spheres which are organized around a parenting arrangement that encourages the female's identification with the place of maternal "holding" and the male's identification with the paternal place of independence.

By shifting the site of individuation from the sphere of the father to that of the mother, *Anywhere But Here* suggests that female individuation need not be achieved by a girl's yielding to the father as a symbol of what she lacks both anatomically and culturally. And perhaps the more profound question posed by this shift is why individuation, as defined by male psychic experience, should constitute a desirable goal for women. Indeed, the very concept of individuality supports the privileging of the masculine in the symbolic order of representation; thus, a selfhood absolute in its individual definition represents, like the father's phallus, woman's devaluation, her lack of agency and autonomy in the social world. Thus, a notion of subjectivity attained only through fixed, unyielding ego boundaries ultimately threatens to defy woman's quest by defining her desire as precisely a lack of desire.

In *Anywhere But Here*, the polarization of gender that is inherent in cultural stereotypes, our notions of the spaces that men and women occupy, is reflected in the two dominant symbols of the novel, houses and cars. While houses represent the protective sphere of maternal stasis, cars suggest the public sphere of motion, the mobility of the father whose authority must eventually break the mother-daughter bond so that the daughter may accept her castration and achieve her full feminine potential through marriage and childbirth. In this context, Ann's confession of the one true love of her mother's life describes the central conflict of women's quests for authentic self-possession. "My mother fell in love with a car" (p. 89). Adele's romance with various automobiles—each one corresponding with a phase of her emotional development—connects her to an American myth passed down from Jay Gatsby to Dean Moriarty, a myth that female heroism redefines. As driver, Adele experiences herself as the subject of her own drives, the active pursuant of desire. The Lincoln Continental, illegitimately purchased with her ex-husband's credit card, represents a vehicle with which to move across psychic and economic boundaries, a vehicle that women lack when they lack a hero. Tired of waiting for a hero, Adele becomes a hero. By stealing a Lincoln Continental, Adele wrests power from the masculine sphere and undermines its symbolic logic. And Ann, watching her mother drive, is offered an empowering image of female mobility and a sense of pride in what she herself may become. "I never wanted to move from my seat. I wanted my mother to keep driving and driving" (p. 90). Indeed, this is not her father's Oldsmobile but her mother's portion of history and wealth, their ticket across the continent.

In spite of its radical innovation of literary form and theme, *Anywhere But Here* is clearly a novel identifiable within a long-standing American tradition of novels of flight and departure. In one sense, Ann and Adele represent the female versions of Leslie Fiedler's "Good Bad Boys," whose flights from responsible adulthood echo America's own reluctant coming of age. According to Fiedler, the

career of the classic "Good Bad Boy" has changed little throughout
the evolution of American fiction: he "begins his revolt by playing
hooky. . . . Similarly, he is allowed still to 'hook' things."[9] In *Anywhere But Here* the Good Bad Girlhood depicted by Simpson is characterized by similar misadventures which nevertheless subvert traditional notions that woman's self-definition is derived essentially
through her "goodness," or through a relational mode that guides
moral development in accordance with a capacity for empathy with
others. In contrast, Ann and Adele act in accordance with their own
spontaneous impulses: "We stole vegetables all across America," recalls Ann, "anything we could eat without cooking" (p. 19). Adele is
not only happy to write Ann's excuse from school, she convinces her
to play hooky so that they can purchase bingo tickets at Red Owl
supermarkets all over Wisconsin. Ann remembers a brief period
when they both worked at a Los Angeles clothing store and shop-
lifted thousands of dollars worth of goods. Says Ann, "It didn't feel
like stealing exactly. . . . And when we drove home . . . you could
touch the clothes on the car seat next to you and feel like you'd gotten something out of the day . . ." (p. 303).

Anywhere But Here, like Marilynne Robinson's *Housekeeping*, engages, through a transvaluation of mutually empowering forces, an
essential dialectic of interior and exterior, home and the world. Like
Sylvie, the vagabond aunt in Robinson's novel, Adele's ideal home
is a home capable of expressing meanings that homes are generally
meant to conceal, a home where inside and outside are held in balance. The house where Ann and Adele live with Adele's second husband, Ted, becomes an expression of the tension between close and
open space; Adele's unspoken commitment to keeping the rooms
free of furniture shows her refusal of conventional patterns for representing human comfort and safety. When Ida and Carol's family
come for Thanksgiving dinner, Adele panics; she rents a houseful of
temporary furniture to impress the family, and when it's all set up
she moves from room to room in utter amazement, posing in every
chair, trying out different angles, hoping somehow to work herself
meaningfully into this pattern. But no proper living room ever really
makes her feel alive; no configuration out of *Good Housekeeping* can
ever reveal the truth of her desire to escape rather than create de-
signs symbolic of permanence. Consequently, the only house Adele
truly longs for is the house not hers, the unfound home, the home

whose value is contingent upon its chances of remaining an impossible possession. Adele's attraction to the finest hotels and luxury houses for sale leads her through a series of debts, fraudulent real estate inquiries, and broken leases. These temporary shelters—as fleeting as her romances with men—are more continuous with Adele's sense of dislocation and separation than any home promising to hold people together against the forces of time and desire.

While automobiles represent for Ann and Adele the promise of such discovery, houses determine female destiny and limit female power to the interior place of holding. "Sometimes," says Ann, "when you walk in a house that has been newly, thoroughly cleaned, you feel light. You're eating, you're lounging on a couch, spreading open the pages of a magazine, but you're a small thing, in the rooms. You're living the way people live inside movies" (p. 375). Here Ann sees beneath the illusion of permanence and desireless bliss that is the idealized image of home. While cultural conventions connect women's housekeeping with the cleanliness of an inner space, a cycle of washing away and purging oneself of desire, a house, Ann realizes, is always an unauthentic expression of desires that operate precisely to break down such barriers and fill the inner space with the outer world.

"Thus an immense cosmic house is a potential of every dream of houses," writes Bachelard. "A house that is as dynamic as this allows the poet to inhabit the universe."[10] Here we find the dream of the author and the authority of woman's desire similarly defined: to create a merger of the internal and external sphere and to claim this sphere, finally, as the place of creativity and self-discovery. Woman's quest is thus defined as the search for imaginative structures capable of expressing a pattern that conventional images of home cannot contain: the dream of desire beyond the sphere of the mother, beyond the limits of housekeeping.

In *Anywhere But Here*, the psychic longings to transcend domesticity and at the same time maintain the network of family relationships is worked out in the psychic space where the developmental paths of parents and children overlap. This arena of constant negotiation is never more safe than it is dangerous, never more life-giving than annihilating. Simpson dramatizes this duality most powerfully in patterns of holding and purging, patterns that describe the collision of opposing forces which the female quest must ultimately embrace. In *Anywhere But Here* these forces of attachment and separation mobilize the cycle of female desire as the women of Simpson's novel alternately cleanse themselves of need and then fill up with it again.

"We fought," says Ann. "When my mother and I crossed state lines . . . I wouldn't even look at her. I knew how to make her suffer" (p. 2). When their arguments become too much for her, Adele pulls off the highway and tells Ann to get out the car if she is so miserable. Ann gets out and feeds her senses on these new, strange surroundings. "It was always a shock the first minute because nothing outside was bad. I stood there at first amazed that there was nothing horrible in the landscape." Ann then watches as Adele slams the gas pedal and goes on without her, driving until mother and daughter can perceive one another only as "dots in the distance." At this point, Ann bursts into tears; Adele stops driving, turns the car around, and returns for her daughter. Ann recalls, "It did something for my mother, every time she let me off the highway and then came back and I was there. She was proving something to herself. When she drove back, she'd be nodding, grateful-looking, as if we had another chance, as if something had been washed out of her" (p. 15). This ritual cleansing of desire that conditions the sphere of feminine activity is expressed also by Adele's sister, Carol, shortly following the accidental death of her son, Ben. Struggling to comprehend this new, vast space that has come between them, Carol takes into her hands a rock that Ben had kept in his room. This mineral mass once existed for Ben as he had existed for Carol: they were both prized possessions, symbols of their permanent place in the world. Recalling the moment when she discovered the rock in Ben's room, Carol says, "I understood then the way I don't anymore about religion. It is a matter of concentration, a promise never to let anything else come between. I had that kind of bond then . . . trying to clean yourself out, so you're an empty house, a dustless vessel" (p. 347). Carol's promise "never to let anything else come between" echoes Adele's promise to her daughter, spoken after Adele's sudden breakup with a boyfriend who tried to interfere in one of her arguments with Ann: "No one, not anyone, can get between us" (p. 196). Here Adele, like Carol, establishes a moment of communion not only with Ann but with a vision of herself as essentially both mother *and* child, identities never entirely separate in the psychic lives of women. Carol and

Adele's promises, however, are very different in that Carol's promise calls upon a force perhaps greater than what is in this world, while Adele's promise calls upon a child to answer a need that no child could be expected to fulfill. Yet both sisters attain, briefly, the absence of all worldly desire that is the metaphysical aim of keeping houses and keeping children. To empty oneself entirely of longing is to fashion the inner space so that it corresponds to a sacred structure characterized by the absence of desire. To make of this inner space a church is to support a sanctified image of the father's house—and of woman—as spaces which must be systematically swept clean of all untidy conflicts of possessiveness, sexual longing, and longing for agency in the pursuit of one's own desires.

Perhaps, then, it is a naive misreading of woman's desire not to desire that lurks behind the question "What *does* she want?" "We wanted too many things," Ann laments. "I didn't want to leave, but I didn't want to give up California, either" (p. 86). In this conflict the dream of the poet and the poetics of female desire share a common goal: to create a union of the internal and external sphere and to claim this inclusive territory, finally, as the place of creativity and self-discovery. Woman's quest is thus defined as the search for imaginative structures capable of supporting the paradox that "in being with the other, I may experience the most profound sense of self," just as in transience one may experience the most profound sense of home.[11]

The shifting of female imagination from the site of stasis and containment to transience and emergence parallels a shift that Donald Marshall has observed in recent novelistic patterns from the male "plot of history" to the feminist "plot of discovery," the former characterized by a "structured relationship of beginning and end," the latter not defined by one dominant reality but by a commitment to a process of shared interpretation between subjects, a process that constantly seeks out new interpretive possibilities as it avoids topo-analytical determinacy.[12]

According to Jessica Benjamin, a new interpretive possibility exists in "intersubjectivity." Simpson's novel demonstrates the potential of the intersubjective mode to support a feminist plot of shared discovery. As Lee Edwards observes in *Psyche As Hero*, "From fictions fascinated by the need for daughters to escape their crippled and crippling mothers, we move to tales concerned with figures who are themselves both mother and daughter."[13] Through the interweaving of such figures, *Anywhere But Here* presents a radical challenge to the myth of the solitary hero enacting a solitary quest for the good of his community. In the commingling of equally subjective first-person female narrators, voices related yet distinct, Simpson's novel speaks across boundaries of fixed heroism as Ann, Adele, Carol, and Ida address one another in a collective search for individual value and an individual search for family identity. Female self-definition is thus perceived as a process of transmission among women. All share a common occasion for speaking, a common quest and a common question. What is achieved is a harmony of voices interacting in the creation of collective remembrance. The communication that occurs among subjects invites participation in the transformation of interpretive schemas, establishing what may be envisioned as a community for the shaping of new literary and cultural conventions. Thus, as Frye notes, "representation can be claimed in a voice among other voices, a female 'I' speaking to other women and building shared perspectives as mutual outsiders to the dominant culture."[14]

In this particular sense, Simpson's novel offers a challenging view for feminist criticism at the end of the 1980s as the next generation of feminist authors and critics—many of whom were spiritually mothered by feminists of the 1960s and 1970s—shifts gears to suit new terrain, reconsidering previous patterns in light of new spaces; emphasizing new theories alongside venerable practices; challenging former convictions now believed untenable; and, inevitably, parting company with those teachers in whose eyes we once thought we glimpsed an image of our future selves. No doubt there is still much to learn from the tales of quests that changed so many women's lives, stories that gave voice, at last, to the search for our mother's gardens. But it is not surprising that the daughters now contemplating their own heroic options should hunger for something more than what these plots could yield. And so the quest begins again, but this time with a new question: What if *I am* my mother's garden? How do I go about unearthing myself from her soil to claim my own ground?

Anywhere But Here may be read to support Chodorow's conclusion in *The Reproduction of Mothering.* Even while literary conventions are changing as a result of the outpouring of women's writings over the last few decades, and even while feminist criticism has suggested the possibility of searching out new cognitive modes with which to represent women's lives, an image of true female mobility remains ultimately conditional to women's cultural identity as mothers. As long as there remains a capitalist industrial system founded on a firm division between the sexes, the spaces that men and women occupy, it is likely that women will remain the primary source of mothering. Consequently, their daughters are likely to reproduce the split in gender identification and continue operating predominantly in a relational mode based on maternal-filial sameness.[15]

Anywhere But Here is as much concerned with Adele's coming of age as with Ann's. The maturation of woman is defined as a process not necessarily reliant upon individuation but as one that brings both mother and father into view as agents and subjects of their own desire. In both spheres the truly autonomous subject is the one able to move between separateness and connectedness, forces which mutually advance progress and participation in the world. In *Anywhere But Here* intersubjective growth is a shared process that occurs between a searching self and supportive others. What Ann inherits through the matriarchal line is a capacity for recognizing this process in recipes, houses, shopping malls, meals—all compositional structures that express both unity and fragmentation. But what Ann also inherits is a relational subjectivity that does not hinder her development; rather, it makes her growth an occasion for communal growth and awakening. The female community represented by the novel's narrative form indicates history in formation through the process of women speaking to one another, telling each other their stories, enacting their heroic quest(s) together. When Ann leaves home and finds her own place in the world, Adele, too, begins to accept both her own limits and the limits of others. The novel's last words are hers, indicating this awareness: "You carry a baby in the womb for nine months and then, when they're grown up, they call you collect, when they remember. She has her own life. And that's okay. I've learned to be patient. . . . The ups and downs; I live with it. And I've got a lot ahead of me and a lot to be proud of. I know: she is the reason I was born" (p. 406).

At the conclusion of *Anywhere But Here*, Ann moves east to attend college, fixing herself and her mother at opposite extremes of the country they once traveled together. Yet mother and daughter remain held in tension by a common need to negotiate a safe territory where they can be alone in the presence of one another. And finally they do arrive here through their mediation in a struggle toward emotional and psychological maturity that has shifted from the patriarchal to the matriarchal arena, a struggle fought both individually and communally. The historical shift to the matriarchal line introduces a new region for the portrayal of female experience. To explore this region is to hope for eventual balance between the close and the far, the here and the anywhere but here. The potential of a cognitive strategy formulated through spatial metaphors to alter the ways women represent their lives is reflected in Ann's desire to discover a future in memories of the past, a self in the presence of the other, and, at last, a home in the world: "My mother and I should have both been girls who stayed out on the porch a little longer than the rest, girls who strained to hear the long-distance trucks on the highway and who listened to them, not the nearer crickets. We would have been girls who had names in their heads: Ann Arbor, Chicago, Cheyenne, San Francisco, Portland, Honolulu, Los Angeles; girls who looked at the sky and wanted to go away" (p. 48).

8. Conclusion

Radical Departures

I make my Psyche from my need. And when others need a different Psyche, let them make it. So this is not arche-typos or the first mold, from which all form is cast, transhistorical and transcultural. This myth is made in time. —DUPLESSIS, "PSYCHE, OR WHOLENESS"

At a recent academic conference, I had the good fortune to participate in a session on vagrancy in twentieth-century American women's literature. After the papers were read—all dealing with female authors, female authorship, and all in some way examining the question of whether anything could be "foundationally" female about the texts—the respondent to our papers addressed the audience directly and intelligently, but with a mildly impatient inflection. "We're still talking about men," she said. Her voice was scolding, firm, and she seemed weary of repeating the phrase, as if it had become a sad litany of sorts. And it has. I understand her frustration, and I admit that this study has gotten me into the same kind of trouble. Hence, picking up a cue from Judith Butler and other contemporary gender theorists, my conclusion accepts the inevitability of trouble and the responsibility for finding out the best way to occupy it when responding to the contradictions of a phallogocentric culture.[1]

Certainly, explicit in my analysis are theories, forms, and conventions formulated and postulated by men; the subjects of my analyses are characters and alternative or subversive strategies formulated by women, ostensibly in opposition to the totalizing gestures of masculine discourses and practices. But I cannot speak of a feminine tradition apart from a masculine one without creating my own totalizing structure. Consequently, in proposing to address what is fundamentally and necessarily subversive in contemporary quest-

romances, I run the risk of perpetuating the same oppositional logic
that feminist politics has taught me to regard as highly suspect. As
Butler states, "The problematic circularity of a feminist inquiry into
gender is underscored by the presence of positions which, on the one
hand, presume that gender is a secondary characteristic of persons
and those which, on the other hand, argue that the very notion of the
person . . . is a masculinist construction and prerogative."[2]

So what can one say of women's texts? One might say that women's
texts exist not as sites of a substantive category of woman, but as
culturally specific performative acts that speak from within and *in
relation to* the very complex discursive and material structures that
create the effects of gender identity. In other words, one might say
that the subject of quest-romance does not exist at all. And while I
would remain self-critical of an antifoundationalist position in relation to feminist theory and politics, it appears that there is no outsider position available, no safe place from which to view patriarchy
brooding stoically in its "natural" habitat while I remain critically
detached and observant. So, finally, I have reached my own exas-
peration point, and I will ask once again: what does one do with this
paradox that deconstructs one's purpose before one's eyes?

Feminism in the 1990s must ultimately proceed from this paradox. The essentialist debate, which figures prominently in feminist
scholarship and recent critical attacks on the goal of unity in feminism, does not obstruct the feminization of the quest-romance, as I
understand it, but rather helps describe the sphere of its inquiry:
who are we talking about when we talk about women writing, or
women questing? Indeed, the answer is best expressed in another
question: who haven't we been talking about? Reading women's
quest-romances, one discovers the limitations that both men and
women have had to face in the transformation of normative dialogic
structures. Consequently, I believe that when we read Marilynne
Robinson's novel, we do learn something about the lost fathers of
Housekeeping, just as by reading *Moby Dick* we can learn something
about the women ostensibly on shore, the women whose absence
from the *Pequod* speaks volumes about the relationships of the men
who are present on ship, as well as the socioeconomic relations of
race and class in nineteenth-century American life. My belief is that
woman's quest openly addresses this paradox in its effort to portray
the need for political agency in the quest to expand the limiting

available categories of identity. It is a movement that presumes the existence of variously located agents all touched by a fundamental structural predicament: how to assert identity and at the same time preserve and conduct our powerful capacity to think beyond the fixity of gender and other socially determined conditions. The feminization of quest-romance is evidence of a collective, crosscultural project to reach for inclusiveness in American myth and vision. It suggests a restoration of the literary subject as antiessentialist, historically engaged, and critically self-aware. It is a collaborative quest for a radical reassessment of social identity that will make possible individual survival.

In the contemporary language of new myths, woman *is* the articulation of a contradiction that must effectively be left intact until her next move is known. And in the meantime she is taking us all to new places. Her movement, which I have attempted to elaborate in this project, suggests a vital context for studying American feminism and American literature at this moment in time. This study has explored some of the recent texts and contexts that have contributed to the feminization of the quest. By focusing particularly on contemporary women's writings, I have tried to establish that the feminization of the quest, a project that began discernibly in the nineteenth century, has come to full emergence in the last forty years. Indeed, insofar as literature does intersect with a historical and cultural moment, it seems that the call issued by feminist critics for a new portrayal of women "lighting out" is at last getting a response. Psyche's torch is lighted: the rejuvenation of contemporary culture depends as much on challenging the notion of coherent subjectivity as it has traditionally depended on the development of the coherent subject.

One of the principal functions of feminist criticism has been to reveal how cultural images of women became trapped in negative valuations of the "feminine" as a symbolic category associating gender "difference" with "inferiority." However, the feminization of the quest does not focus on woman's entrapment in but on her emergence from categorical "otherness." While feminist criticism has often assumed the task of exposing the obstacles and impediments that have problematized women's literary representations, the feminization of the quest indicates that a shift from passivity to action, from stasis to progress, from theory to practice is informing women's writing.

Indeed, the very history and process of women's quests indicates a way of thinking critically as well as a way of continuing to do feminist criticism at a time when many of us are trying to incorporate feminist practices into a more encompassing cultural context. Just as women's quests lead them both deeper into the self and into more active involvement with the world, feminist criticism leads the critic into an exploration of what forces ultimately constitute the self and the text, and the self *in relation to* the text. This process has the potential to affirm a basic plurality in the interpretive process and in the cultural context within which interpretation operates.

To what time-specific needs does the feminization of quest-romance respond? Psyche begins, as all heroes begin, with a call to "light out," but the call is predicated upon a distinct illumination of history. "The social recognition of the hero depends precisely on society's recognition of its own unhappiness," writes Lee Edwards.[3] Woman makes her Psyche, each from her own need, but all emerging from a time of heightened historical and cultural awareness. Society makes its hero, also from its needs, but necessarily emerging from its fascination with and skepticism about the individual subject. The postmodern quest provides no solution to the problem of validating the subject as woman, but it does indicate a historical juncture of woman's time and a materialist philosophical account of socially instituted heroism. The feminization of the quest provides a frame for drawing a diversity of cultural experience into the currency of signification. It is not simply an inverse of masculine norms, but a questioning of the presupposed categories of gender. In this way, women's quests affirm their active part in generating social awareness on both a personal and public level.

Thus, extending Jessica Benjamin's analysis, an understanding of woman's fluid object-relational structures opens a door to social intersubjectivity, a mode of being *and* a mode of being together. As a social paradigm, intersubjectivity reflects Judith Butler's notion of coalitional politics as "a set of dialogic encounters by which variously positioned women articulate separate identities within the framework of an emergent coalition."[4] Like the intersubjective mode, antifoundationalist coalitions enable a balance between selves and others, a balance where no community precludes another but ultimately understands itself and its own interworkings in relation to other communities.

This coalitional tension remains one of the foremost themes of the American experience, and representing this theme remains one of the primary objects of American literature. The American literary imagination draws us constantly into questions of who actually defines the American subject; at its heart are issues of uncertain heroism and unattainable balance between individuals and cultures both indelibly marked and measured by differences of sex, race, class, religion, region, experience, human capacity. We are overwhelmed by a longing to be a part of an all-encompassing experience, and we are equally overwhelmed by a fear of losing the very substance of our Americaness—ourselves—by virtue of this longing. In its awareness of such longings and fears, in its resistance to the necessary processes of self-definition, the American subject and the American quest is perpetually recovered, lost and redefined as essentially on the move.

Consequently, when we read of women's quests, we become pioneers ourselves, drawn into unnamed regions by processes of imagination that challenge and expand our own psychic possibilities, our own potential as heroes. The remaking of Psyche is a project for cultures as well as individuals. It is humanity's quest to explore and understand collectively the myths we have only half seen and the powers we have only half realized. Through our participation in the remaking of Psyche, we come to recognize that the feminization of quest-romance is no less than the feminization of culture, and no greater than our individual capacities to truly recognize and love one another.

Notes

1. Introduction: The Feminization of Quest-Romance

1. Joseph Campbell, *The Hero with a Thousand Faces*, p. 116.
2. Ibid.
3. Annis Pratt, *Archetypal Patterns in Women's Fiction*, pp. 3–7.
4. C. G. Jung, *Symbols of Transformation: An Analysis of the Prelude to a Case of Schizophrenia*, p. 333.
5. Missy Dehn Kubitschek, "Paule Marshall's Women on Quest," *Black American Literary Forum* 21 (Spring–Summer 1987): 227.
6. Campbell, *The Hero with a Thousand Faces*, p. 384.
7. Ibid., p. 352.
8. Marlon B. Ross, "Romantic Quest and Conquest: Troping Masculine Power in the Crisis of Poetic Identity," in *Romanticism and Feminism*, ed. Anne K. Mellor, p. 41.
9. Northrop Frye, *Anatomy of Criticism: Four Essays*, p. 322.
10. Ibid., pp. 193, 322–323.
11. Campbell, *The Hero with a Thousand Faces*, p. 136.
12. Ross, "Romantic Quest and Conquest," p. 31.
13. Harold Bloom, "The Internalization of Quest-Romance," in *Romanticism and Consciousness: Essays in Criticism*, ed. Harold Bloom, p. 15.
14. Ibid., p. 12.
15. Ross, "Romantic Quest and Conquest," p. 28.
16. Pratt, *Archetypal Patterns*, p. 6.
17. Richard Chase, *The American Novel and Its Tradition*, pp. 6–7.
18. Ibid., p. 11.
19. Ibid., p. 7.

20. Judith Fetterly, *The Resisting Reader: A Feminist Approach to American Fiction*, p. xii.

21. Ihab Hassan, *Radical Innocence: Studies in the Contemporary American Novel*, p. 111.

22. Bloom, "The Internalization of Quest-Romance," p. 3. Bloom ascribes the mapping of the psyche to Blake, Wordsworth, and Freud.

23. Carol Christ, *Diving Deep and Surfacing: Women Writers on Spiritual Quest*, p. 9.

24. Lee R. Edwards, "The Labors of Psyche: Toward a Theory of Female Heroism," *Critical Inquiry* 6 (1979): 44.

25. Rachel M. Brownstein, *Becoming a Heroine: Reading about Women in Novels*, pp. 82–83.

26. Katherine Dalsimer, *Female Adolescence: Psychoanalytic Reflections on Works of Literature*, p. 28.

27. Susan J. Rosowski, "The Novel of Awakening," in *The Voyage In: Fictions of Female Development*, ed. Elizabeth Abel, Marianne Hirsch, and Elizabeth Langland, p. 49.

28. Rachel Blau DuPlessis, "Psyche, or Wholeness," *Massachusetts Review* 20 (1979): 94.

29. Betty Friedan, *The Feminine Mystique*, p. 46.

30. Quoted in Barbara A. White, *Growing Up Female: Adolescent Girlhood in American Fiction*, p. 61.

31. Fetterly, *The Resisting Reader*, p. xxii.

32. This passage was brought to light for me by Maureen Ryan, *Innocence and Estrangement in the Fiction of Jean Stafford*, p. 2.

33. Lee R. Edwards, *Psyche as Hero: Female Heroism and Fictional Form*, p. 16.

34. Kim Chernin, *Reinventing Eve: Modern Woman in Search of Herself*, p. 64.

35. Friedan, *The Feminine Mystique*, p. 79.

36. Ntozake Shange, *Betsey Brown*, p. 117.

37. Toril Moi, ed., *The Kristeva Reader*, p. 93.

38. Christ, *Diving Deep and Surfacing*, p. 26.

39. Christ articulates this distinction in ibid., p. 7.

40. Carol Gilligan, *In a Different Voice: Psychological Theory and Women's Development*, p. 148.

41. See DuPlessis, "Psyche, or Wholeness," p. 90.

2. Remaking Psyche

1. Christ, *Diving Deep and Surfacing*, p. 7.

2. Erich Neumann, *Amor and Psyche: The Psychic Development of the Feminine*, trans. Ralph Manheim, p. 85.

3. Ibid., p. 82.

4. Edwards, "The Labors of Psyche," p. 45.

5. Campbell, *The Hero with a Thousand Faces*, p. 389.

6. Edwards, *Psyche as Hero*, p. 4.

7. Jane Tompkins, Afterword to *The Wide Wide World*, by Susan Warner, p. 585.

8. Nina Baym, Introduction to *The Lamplighter*, by Maria Susanna Cummins, p. x.

9. Ibid., p. xix.

10. Ibid.

11. Tompkins, Afterword to *The Wide Wide World*, p. 593.

12. Fetterly, *The Resisting Reader*, p. xvi.

13. Edwards, *Psyche as Hero*, p. 16.

14. Brownstein, *Becoming a Heroine*, p. xv.

15. Jessica Benjamin, "A Desire of One's Own: Psychoanalytic Feminism and Intersubjective Space," in *Feminist Studies/Critical Studies*, ed. Teresa de Lauretis, p. 92.

16. Ibid., p. 93.

17. Domna C. Stanton, "Autogynography: Is the Subject Different?" in *The Female Autograph: Theory and Practice of Autobiography from the Tenth to the Twentieth Century*, ed. Domna C. Stanton, p. 14.

18. Chernin, *Reinventing Eve*, p. 9.

19. Ibid., p. 15.

20. Ibid., pp. 68, 77.

21. DuPlessis, "Psyche, or Wholeness," p. 91.

22. Cited in Geoffrey H. Hartman, *Saving the Text: Literature/Derrida/Philosophy*, pp. 151–152.

23. Donna Haraway, "A Manifesto for Cyborgs: Science, Technology, and Socialist Feminism in the 1980s," *Socialist Review* 80 (1985): 101.

24. My gratitude to Donna Haraway for helping me clarify this point during our session on women and science at the 1989 conference of the Society for Literature and Science at the University of Michigan, Ann Arbor.

25. Evelyn Fox Keller, "Making Gender Visible in the Pursuit of Nature's Secrets," in *Feminist Studies/Critical Studies*, ed. Teresa de Lauretis.

26. Luce Irigaray, *This Sex Which Is Not One*, p. 29.

27. Natalie M. Rosinsky, *Feminist Futures: Contemporary Women's Speculative Fiction*, pp. 29–30.

28. Joanna Russ, *The Female Man*, p. 206.

3. Remembering Molly: Jean Stafford's *The Mountain Lion*

1. Jean Stafford, Author's Note to *The Mountain Lion*, p. xix. Subsequent references to this edition are cited parenthetically in the text.

2. Blanche H. Gelfant, "Revolutionary Turnings: *The Mountain Lion* Reread," in *The Voyage In: Fictions of Female Development*, ed. Elizabeth Abel, Marianne Hirsch, and Elizabeth Langland, p. 150.

3. Hassan, *Radical Innocence*, pp. 118–123.

4. Chase, *The American Novel*, pp. 6–7.

5. Stuart L. Burns, "Counterpoint in Jean Stafford's *The Mountain Lion*," Critique 9 (1967): 31.

6. Melody Graulich, "Jean Stafford's Western Childhood: Huck Finn Joins the Camp Fire Girls," *Denver Quarterly* 18 (1983): 40–41.

7. Gelfant, "Revolutionary Turnings," pp. 159, 149.

8. Rosowski, "The Novel of Awakening," p. 49.

9. Ryan, *Innocence and Estrangement*, p. 50.

10. Fetterly, *The Resisting Reader*, p. xxi.

11. Joanne S. Frye, *Living Stories, Telling Lies: Women and the Novel in Contemporary Experience*, pp. 3–4.

12. Graulich, "Jean Stafford's Western Childhood," p. 47.

13. Barbara A. White, "Initiation, the West, and the Hunt in Jean Stafford's *The Mountain Lion*," *Essays in Literature* 9 (1982): 208.

14. Christ, *Diving Deep and Surfacing*, p. 15.

15. White, "Initiation, the West, and the Hunt," p. 202.

16. Friedan, *The Feminine Mystique*, p. 43.

17. Ibid., p. 46.

18. Gelfant, "Revolutionary Turnings," p. 154.

19. Edwards, *Psyche as Hero*, p. 60.

4. "A Kind of Quest": Mary McCarthy's *Memories of a Catholic Girlhood*

1. Alfred Kazin, "The Self as History: Reflections on Autobiography," in *Telling Lives: The Biographer's Art*, ed. Marc Pachter, p. 76.

2. Albert E. Stone, *Autobiographical Occasions and Original Acts: Versions of American Identity from Henry Adams to Nate Shaw*, p. 196.

3. Ibid.

4. Ibid., p. 195.

5. Lynn Z. Bloom, "Promises Fulfilled: Positive Images of Women in Twentieth-Century Autobiography," in *Feminist Criticism: Essays in Theory, Poetry, and Prose*, ed. Cheryl Brown and Karen Olson, p. 334.

6. Patricia Meyer Spacks, "Reflecting Women," *Yale Review* 63 (October 1973): 39.

7. Stone, *Autobiographical Occasions*, p. 229.

8. Cited in Sandra C. M. Gilbert and Susan D. D. Gubar, "Ceremonies of the Alphabet: Female Grandmatologies and the Female Autograph," in

The Female Autograph: Theory and Practice of Autobiography from the Tenth to the Twentieth Century, ed. Domna C. Stanton, p. 43.

9. John Paul Eakin, *Fictions in Autobiography: Studies in the Art of Self-Invention,* p. 43.

10. Mary McCarthy, *Memories of a Catholic Girlhood,* p. 3. Subsequent references to this edition are cited parenthetically in the text.

11. Frye, *Living Stories, Telling Lives,* p. 57.

12. Spacks, "Reflecting Women," p. 46.

13. Mary McCarthy, "The Art of Fiction," *Paris Review* 27 (Winter–Spring 1962): 81.

14. Eileen Simpson, *Orphans: Real and Imaginary,* p. 17.

15. Rosalie Hewitt, "A 'Home Address for the Self': Mary McCarthy's Autobiographical Journey," *Journal of Narrative Technique* 12 (Spring 1982): 103.

16. Frye, *Living Stories, Telling Lives,* p. 64.

17. Estelle C. Jelinek, *The Tradition of Women's Autobiography: From Antiquity to the Present,* p. 187.

18. Christ, *Diving Deep and Surfacing,* p. 11.

19. Michael Ragussis, *Acts of Naming: The Family Plot in Fiction,* p. 13.

20. Stanton, "Autogynography," p. 15.

21. Christ, *Diving Deep and Surfacing,* p. 128.

22. Frye, *Living Stories, Telling Lives,* p. 62.

23. Ragussis, *Acts of Naming,* p. 10.

24. Oscar Wilde, "The Critic as Artist," in *The Portable Oscar Wilde,* ed. Richard Aldington and Stanley Weintraub, p. 75.

25. McCarthy, "The Art of Fiction," pp. 93–94.

5. "The Spark from the Outside World":
Anne Moody's *Coming of Age in Mississippi*

1. Mary Helen Washington, "Teaching *Black-Eyed Susans:* An Approach to the Study of Black Women Writers," in *All the Women Are White, All the Blacks Are Men, But Some of Us Are Brave: Black Women's Studies,* ed. Gloria T. Hull, Patricia Bell Scott, and Barbara Smith, p. 212.

2. Ibid., p. 214.

3. Louise Meriwether, *Daddy Was a Numbers Runner,* p. 187.

4. Alice Walker, *In Search of Our Mother's Gardens,* p. 5.

5. Anne Moody, *Coming of Age in Mississippi,* p. 33. Subsequent references to this edition are cited parenthetically in the text.

6. Kimberly W. Benston, "I Yam What I Am: The Topos of Un(nam-

ing) in Afro-American Literature," in *Black Literature and Literary Theory*, ed. Henry Louis Gates, Jr., p. 156.

7. Ibid., p. 152.

8. Gloria T. Hull, Introduction to *All the Women Are White, All the Blacks Are Men, But Some of Us Are Brave: Black Women's Studies*, ed. Gloria T. Hull, Patricia Bell Scott, and Barbara Smith, p. xvii.

9. Benston, "I Yam What I Am," p. 153.

10. Sondra O'Neale, "Inhibiting Midwives, Usurping Creators: The Struggling Emergence of Black Women in American Fiction," in *Feminist Studies: Critical Studies*, ed. Teresa de Lauretis, pp. 143–144.

11. Christ, *Diving Deep and Surfacing*, p. 23.

12. Trudier Harris, *From Mammies to Militants: Domestics in Black American Literature*, p. 12.

13. Ibid., p. 19.

14. Washington's comment is found in Hull, Introduction to *All the Women Are White*, p. xv.

15. Gerda Lerner, ed., *Black Women in White America: A Documentary History*, p. 163.

16. O'Neale, "Inhibiting Midwives, Usurping Creators," p. 144.

17. Stephen Butterfield, *Black Autobiography in America*, p. 216.

18. Toni Morrison, *The Bluest Eye*, p. 43.

19. Mary Helen Washington, "Teaching *Black-Eyed Susans*," p. 214.

20. Ntozake Shange, *for colored girls who have considered suicide when the rainbow is enuf*, p. 63.

21. O'Neale, "Inhibiting Midwives, Usurping Creators," p. 140.

22. Walker, *In Search of Our Mother's Gardens*, p. 126.

6. "Happily at Ease in the Dark": Marilynne Robinson's *Housekeeping*

1. Elizabeth A. Meese, *Crossing the Double-Cross: The Practice of Feminist Criticism*, p. 68.

2. Maureen Ryan, "Marilynne Robinson's *Housekeeping*: The Subversive Narrative and the New American Eve," p. 68.

3. Marilynne Robinson, *Housekeeping*, p. 214. Subsequent references to this edition are cited parenthetically in the text.

4. Pratt, *Archetypal Patterns in Women's Fiction*, p. 70.

5. Hassan, *Radical Innocence*, p. 336.

6. Roberta Rubenstein, *Boundaries of the Self: Gender, Culture, Fiction*, p. 227.

7. Ryan, "Marilynne Robinson's *Housekeeping*," p. 6.

8. Meese, *Crossing the Double-Cross*, p. 62.

9. Frye, *Living Stories, Telling Lives*, p. 45.

10. Gaston Bachelard, *The Poetics of Reverie: Childhood, Language, and the Cosmos*, p. 100.

11. Nor Hall, *The Moon and the Virgin: Reflections on the Archetypal Feminine*, p. 24.

7. Shifting Gears:
Mona Simpson's *Anywhere But Here*

1. Benjamin, "A Desire of One's Own," p. 97.

2. Mona Simpson, *Anywhere But Here*, pp. 90, 2. Subsequent references to this edition are cited parenthetically in the text.

3. Gaston Bachelard, *The Poetics of Space*, p. 8.

4. Benjamin, "A Desire of One's Own," p. 87.

5. Nancy Chodorow, *The Reproduction of Mothering: Psychoanalysis and the Sociology of Gender*, p. 87.

6. Ibid., p. 100.

7. Erik H. Erikson, "Womanhood and the Inner Space," in *Identity Youth and Crisis*, p. 270.

8. Benjamin, "A Desire of One's Own," p. 91.

9. Leslie Fiedler, *Love and Death in the American Novel*, p. 289.

10. Bachelard, *The Poetics of Space*, p. 51.

11. Benjamin, "A Desire of One's Own," p. 92.

12. Quoted in Frye, *Living Stories, Telling Lives*, p. 40.

13. Edwards, *Psyche as Hero*, pp. 240–241.

14. Frye, *Living Stories, Telling Lives*, p. 60.

15. Chodorow, *The Reproduction of Mothering*, p. 212.

8. Conclusion: Radical Departures

1. Judith Butler, *Gender Trouble: Feminism and the Subversion of Identity*, p. ix.

2. Ibid., p. 11.

3. Edwards, "The Labors of Psyche," p. 34.

4. Butler, *Gender Trouble*, p. 14.

Bibliography

Bachelard, Gaston. *The Poetics of Reverie: Childhood, Language, and the Cosmos.* Trans. Daniel Russell. Boston: Beacon Press, 1969.

———. *The Poetics of Space.* Trans. Maria Jolas. Boston: Beacon Press, 1964.

Baym, Nina. Introduction to *The Lamplighter,* by Maria Susanna Cummins. New Brunswick: Rutgers University Press, 1988.

Beauvoir, Simone de. *The Second Sex.* Trans. H. M. Parshley. New York: Vintage Books, 1952.

Benjamin, Jessica. "A Desire of One's Own: Psychoanalytic Feminism and Intersubjective Space." In *Feminist Studies/Critical Studies,* ed. Teresa de Lauretis, pp. 78–101. Bloomington: Indiana University Press, 1986.

Benston, Kimberly W. "I Yam What I Am: The Topos of Un(naming) in Afro-American Literature." In *Black Literature and Literary Theory,* ed. Henry Louis Gates, Jr., pp. 151–172. New York: Methuen, 1984.

Bloom, Harold. "The Internalization of Quest-Romance." In *Romanticism and Consciousness: Essays in Criticism,* ed. Harold Bloom, pp. 3–23. New York: W. W. Norton, 1970.

Bloom, Lynn Z. "Promises Fulfilled: Positive Images of Women in Twentieth-Century Autobiography." In *Feminist Criticism: Essays in Theory, Poetry, and Prose,* ed. Cheryl Brown and Karen Olson, pp. 324–338. Metuchen, N.J.: Scarecrow Press, 1978.

Brownstein, Rachel M. *Becoming a Heroine: Reading about Women in Novels.* New York: Penguin Books, 1982.

Burns, Stuart L. "Counterpoint in Jean Stafford's *The Mountain Lion.*" *Critique* 9 (1967): 20–32.

Butler, Judith. *Gender Trouble: Feminism and the Subversion of Identity.* New York: Routledge, 1990.

Butterfield, Stephen. *Black Autobiography in America.* Amherst: University of Massachusetts Press, 1974.

Campbell, Joseph. *The Hero with a Thousand Faces.* Princeton: Princeton University Press, 1949.

Chase, Richard. *The American Novel and Its Tradition.* Baltimore: Johns Hopkins University Press, 1957.

Chernin, Kim. *Reinventing Eve: Modern Woman in Search of Herself.* New York: Harper and Row, 1987.

Chodorow, Nancy. *The Reproduction of Mothering: Psychoanalysis and the Sociology of Gender.* Berkeley: University of California Press, 1978.

Christ, Carol. *Diving Deep and Surfacing: Women Writers on Spiritual Quest.* 2nd ed. Boston: Beacon Press, 1980.

Cixous, Hélène. "Castration or Decapitation?" Trans. Annette Kuhn. *Signs* 7 (1981): 41–55.

Dalsimer, Katherine. *Female Adolescence: Psychoanalytic Reflections on Works of Literature.* New Haven: Yale University Press, 1986.

DuPlessis, Rachel Blau. "Psyche, or Wholeness." *Massachusetts Review* 20 (1979): 77–96.

Eakin, John Paul. *Fictions in Autobiography: Studies in the Art of Self-Invention.* Princeton: Princeton University Press, 1985.

Edwards, Lee R. "The Labors of Psyche: Toward a Theory of Female Heroism." *Critical Inquiry* 6 (1979): 33–49.

———. *Psyche as Hero: Female Heroism and Fictional Form.* Middletown, Conn.: Wesleyan University Press, 1984.

Erikson, Erik H. "Womanhood and the Inner Space." In *Identity Youth and Crisis,* pp. 261–294. New York: W. W. Norton, 1968.

Fetterly, Judith. *The Resisting Reader: A Feminist Approach to American Fiction.* Bloomington: Indiana University Press, 1978.

Fiedler, Leslie. *Love and Death in the American Novel.* Rev. ed. New York: Stein and Day, 1966.

Friedan, Betty. *The Feminine Mystique.* 1963. Reprint. New York: Dell, 1983.

Frye, Joanne S. *Living Stories, Telling Lives: Women and the Novel in Contemporary Experience.* Ann Arbor: University of Michigan Press, 1986.

Frye, Northrop. *Anatomy of Criticism: Four Essays.* Princeton: Princeton University Press, 1957.

Fryer, Judith. *Felicitous Space: The Imaginative Structures of Edith Wharton and Willa Cather.* Chapel Hill: University of North Carolina Press, 1986.

Gelfant, Blanche H. "Revolutionary Turnings: *The Mountain Lion* Reread." In *The Voyage In: Fictions of Female Development*, ed. Elizabeth Abel, Marianne Hirsch, and Elizabeth Langland, pp. 149–160. Hanover: University Press of New England, 1983.

Gilbert, Sandra C. M. and Susan D. D. Gubar. "Ceremonies of the Alphabet: Female Grandmatologies and the Female Autograph." In *The Female Autograph: Theory and Practice of Autobiography from the Tenth to the Twentieth Century*, ed. Domna C. Stanton, pp. 21–48. Chicago: University of Chicago Press, 1984.

————. *The Madwoman in the Attic: The Woman Writer and the Nineteenth-Century Literary Imagination*. New Haven: Yale University Press, 1979.

Gilligan, Carol. *In a Different Voice: Psychological Theory and Women's Development*. Cambridge: Harvard University Press, 1982.

Graulich, Melody. "Jean Stafford's Western Childhood: Huck Finn Joins the Camp Fire Girls." *Denver Quarterly* 18 (1983): 39–55.

Hall, Nor. *The Moon and the Virgin: Reflections on the Archetypal Feminine*. New York: Harper and Row, 1980.

Haraway, Donna. "A Manifesto for Cyborgs: Science, Technology, and Socialist Feminism in the 1980s." *Socialist Review* 80 (1985): 65–107.

————. "Situated Knowledges: The Science Question in Feminism and the Privilege of Partial Perspective." *Feminist Studies* 14 (1988): 575–599.

Harris, Trudier. *From Mammies to Militants: Domestics in Black American Literature*. Philadelphia: Temple University Press, 1982.

Hartman, Geoffrey H. *Saving the Text: Literature/Derrida/Philosophy*. Baltimore: Johns Hopkins University Press, 1981.

Hassan, Ihab H. "Jean Stafford: The Expense of Style and the Scope of Sensibility." *Western Review* 19 (1955): 185–203.

————. *Radical Innocence: Studies in the Contemporary American Novel*. Princeton: Princeton University Press, 1961.

Hewitt, Rosalie. "A 'Home Address for the Self': Mary McCarthy's Autobiographical Journey." *Journal of Narrative Technique* 12 (Spring 1982): 95–104.

Hull, Gloria T., Patricia Bell Scott, and Barbara Smith, eds. *All the Women Are White, All the Blacks Are Men, But Some of Us Are Brave: Black Women's Studies*. New York: Feminist Press, 1982.

Irigaray, Luce. *This Sex Which Is Not One*. Trans. Catherine Porter. Ithaca: Cornell University Press, 1985.

Jelinek, Estelle C. *The Tradition of Women's Autobiography: From Antiquity to the Present*. Boston: Twayne Publishers, 1986.

Jung, C. G. *Symbols of Transformation: An Analysis of the Prelude to a Case of Schizophrenia*. 2nd ed., trans. R. F. C. Hull. Princeton: Princeton University Press, 1956.

Kazin, Alfred. "The Self as History: Reflections on Autobiography." In
    Telling Lives: The Biographer's Art, ed. Marc Pachter, pp. 74–89. Phila-
    delphia: University of Pennsylvania Press, 1981.

Keller, Evelyn Fox. "Making Gender Visible in the Pursuit of Nature's Se-
    crets." In *Feminist Studies/Critical Studies*, ed. Teresa de Lauretis,
    pp. 67–77. Bloomington: Indiana University Press, 1986.

Kubitschek, Missy Dehn. "Paule Marshall's Women on Quest." *Black
    American Literary Forum* 21 (Spring–Summer 1987): 43–60.

Lerner, Gerda, ed. *Black Women in White America: A Documentary History*.
    New York: Vintage, 1972.

McCarthy, Mary. "The Art of Fiction." *Paris Review* 27 (Winter–Spring
    1962): 58–94.

———. *Memories of a Catholic Girlhood*. San Diego: Harcourt Brace
    Jovanovich, 1957.

Meese, Elizabeth A. *Crossing the Double-Cross: The Practice of Feminist
    Criticism*. Chapel Hill: University of North Carolina Press, 1986.

Meriwether, Louise. *Daddy Was a Numbers Runner*. Foreword by James
    Baldwin. New York: Jove, 1970.

Moi, Toril, ed. *The Kristeva Reader*. New York: Columbia University Press,
    1986.

Moody, Anne. *Coming of Age in Mississippi*. New York: Dell Publishing
    Co., 1968.

Morrison, Toni. *The Bluest Eye*. New York: Pocket Books, 1970.

Neumann, Erich. *Amor and Psyche: The Psychic Development of the Femi-
    nine*. Trans. Ralph Manheim. Princeton: Princeton University Press,
    1956.

O'Neale, Sondra. "Inhibiting Midwives, Usurping Creators: The Struggling
    Emergence of Black Women in American Fiction." In *Feminist Studies:
    Critical Studies*, ed. Teresa de Lauretis, pp. 139–156. Bloomington: In-
    diana University Press, 1986.

Pratt, Annis, with Barbara White, Andrea Lowenstein, and Mary Wyer.
    Archetypal Patterns in Women's Fiction. Bloomington: Indiana University
    Press, 1981.

Ragussis, Michael. *Acts of Naming: The Family Plot in Fiction*. New York:
    Oxford University Press, 1986.

Robinson, Marilynne. *Housekeeping*. 1980. Reprint. New York: Bantam
    Books, 1982.

Rosinsky, Natalie M. *Feminist Futures: Contemporary Women's Speculative
    Fiction*. Ann Arbor, Mich.: UMI Research Press, 1984.

Rosowski, Susan J. "The Novel of Awakening." In *The Voyage In: Fictions
    of Female Development*, ed. Elizabeth Abel, Marianne Hirsch, and

Elizabeth Langland, pp. 49–68. Hanover: University Press of New England, 1983.

Ross, Marlon B. "Romantic Quest and Conquest: Troping Masculine Power in the Crisis of Poetic Identity." In *Romanticism and Feminism*, ed. Anne K. Mellor, pp. 26–35. Bloomington: Indiana University Press, 1988.

Rubenstein, Roberta. *Boundaries of the Self: Gender, Culture, Fiction.* Urbana: University of Illinois, 1987.

Russ, Joanna. *The Female Man.* Boston: Beacon Press, 1975.

Ryan, Maureen. *Innocence and Estrangement in the Fiction of Jean Stafford.* Baton Rouge: Louisiana State University Press, 1987.

———. "Marilynne Robinson's *Housekeeping:* The Subversive Narrative and the New American Eve." Typescript.

Shange, Ntozake. *Betsey Brown.* New York: St. Martin's Press, 1985.

———. *for colored girls who have considered suicide when the rainbow is enuf.* New York: Macmillan, 1975.

Simpson, Eileen. *Orphans: Real and Imaginary.* New York: New American Library, 1987.

Simpson, Mona. *Anywhere But Here.* New York: Alfred A. Knopf, 1987.

Spacks, Patricia Meyer. "Reflecting Women." *Yale Review* 63 (October 1973): 26–42.

———. "Stages of Self: Notes on Autobiography and the Life Cycle." In *The American Autobiography: A Collection of Critical Essays*, ed. Albert E. Stone, pp. 44–60. Englewood Cliffs, N.J.: Prentice-Hall, 1981.

———. "Women's Stories, Women's Selves." *Hudson Review* 30 (Spring 1977): 29–46.

Stafford, Jean. *The Mountain Lion.* 1947. Reprint. Albuquerque: University of New Mexico Press, 1972.

Stanton, Domna C. "Autogynography: Is the Subject Different?" In *The Female Autograph: Theory and Practice of Autobiography from the Tenth to the Twentieth Century*, ed. Domna C. Stanton, pp. 3–20. Chicago: University of Chicago Press, 1984.

Stone, Albert E. *Autobiographical Occasions and Original Acts: Versions of American Identity from Henry Adams to Nate Shaw.* Philadelphia: University of Pennsylvania Press, 1982.

Tompkins, Jane. Afterword to *The Wide Wide World*, by Susan Warner. New York: Feminist Press, 1987.

Walker, Alice. *In Search of Our Mother's Gardens.* San Diego: Harcourt Brace Jovanovich, 1983.

Washington, Mary Helen. "Teaching *Black-Eyed Susans:* An Approach to the Study of Black Women Writers." In *All the Women Are White, All the*

Blacks Are Men, But Some of Us Are Brave: Black Women's Studies, ed. Gloria T. Hull, Patricia Bell Scott, and Barbara Smith, pp. 208–217. New York: Feminist Press, 1982.

White, Barbara A. *Growing Up Female: Adolescent Girlhood in American Fiction*. Westport, Conn.: Greenwood Press, 1985.

———. "Initiation, the West, and the Hunt in Jean Stafford's *The Mountain Lion*." *Essays in Literature* 9 (1982): 194–210.

Wilde, Oscar. "The Critic as Artist." In *The Portable Oscar Wilde*, ed. Richard Aldington and Stanley Weintraub. New York: Viking Press, 1981.

Index